C000182360

SELLOLOGY

Simplifying the Science of Selling

SELLOLOGY

Simplifying the Science of Selling

Alistaire Jama

KENNEDY ROSS PUBLISHING

SELLOLOGY

Simplifying the Science of Selling

A Kennedy Ross book
First published in Great Britain in 2016
Copyright © Alistaire Jama 2016
All rights reserved.

KENNEDY ROSS PUBLISHING
Preston, UK
www.kennedyross.co.uk

Cover design by Deeper Blue www.wearedeeper.blue
ISBN: 978-0-9954775-1-3

Contents

Introduction

Everything done well in life has a system

.

This book will help you improve your selling skills – Guaranteed

There could be a number of reasons why you've picked up this book or downloaded it, and I believe I can help you with all of them. You may be a sole trader, the CEO of a large-scale corporation, a sales director with a few intractable sales and marketing dilemmas, an apprentice or student with your heart set on a rapid rise in the world of business, or an established salesperson out to re-energise belief in your work.

Whatever your reason, I can help, and over the course of *Sellology: Simplifying the Science of Selling* I set out to do exactly that.

In summary, this book will

- Help you communicate effectively and efficiently so that your sales messages are clearly understood.
- Help you understand, instantly, why you get on with some people and not others when selling, and how to manage this.
- Provide you with planning tools to sell to your customer.
- Teach you the "Magic Question".
- Show you how to connect fully with your customers.
- Show you how to compellingly describe your competitive advantage.
- Explain why "closing" isn't a dirty word.

Before we set out on this journey together — and I'm feeling confident that you will stick with me — do you mind if I ask you a straightforward question? It is the Magic Question I ask whenever I hold a business meeting: What would you like to get from reading this book?

It might just be worth noting down your answer now, then relate that specific problem, troubling doubt or grey area to all that follows as I introduce you to Sellology: Simplifying the Science of Selling and our tried and tested six-step sales system: PROCES (Plan,

Reach, Obtain, Connect, Elaborate, Secure).
So hold on tight, and let's crack on.

Proud to be a salesperson

On an episode of the BBC TV show *The Apprentice: You're Fired!*, a panel member once said, 'This person is such a good salesperson, he could polish a turd.'

Right there is the problem. That – like the other questionable clichés we might hear, such as selling ice to the Eskimos or sand to the Arabs – suggests the epitome of a great salesperson is someone who is on the verge of being a conman. To me, being a good salesperson is about behaving in the best interests of your customer and creating value and impact.

It seems that selling is now perceived poorly as a profession. It evokes images of the kitchen salesman sitting in an elderly couple's house for six hours, insisting at 11.30 p.m. that they sign on the dotted line. Sales people are seen as door knockers trying to sell you something you don't want with the connotation that if I'm selling to you, I'm twisting your arm behind your back and forcing you to buy. This would be putting our interests ahead of our customers', which is bad practice.

My view is that during the years of selling in the land of milk and honey in the UK (2003-2007), we became a nation of order-takers, and forgot the basic principles of sales. In the USA there is a general recognition that sales people are heroes. They drive the economy, they improve profitability, and they connect buyers and sellers. Back in the UK, I recently asked my associates at Kennedy Ross when was the last time they came across somebody with the word "sales" written on their business card or in their job title. It had been a long time, and they had noticed a few euphemistic job titles:

Client Partner
Account Manager
Account Director
Facilitator
Business Development Manager
Engineer
Technical Director

By denying sales as a profession, one denies the fact that it can be conducted brilliantly with a proven system. It means avoiding accountability and ignoring the behaviours required to be a successful salesperson.

So for all of you out there that have been selling successfully — especially those without a recognised and proven sales system — stand up and take a bow. I don't know any other profession that can achieve so much with so little recognised training and support. Imagine what you will achieve now you've found the solution to your problems with *Sellology: Simplifying the Science of Selling*.

In the not so distant good ol' days when a customer needed to buy something, there was a lot less choice available and a lot less information on hand to help the buyer get the best deal. Sales people were often able to make a sale there and then — on the day, at the meeting, over the phone. This has now changed. The evolution of technology has put the power of choice into the hands of the buyer. However, the sales systems that companies rely on to sell their products and services have not really changed.

Good sales people don't con, aren't fakes and tell no lies to make their sales. What they do have is a robust system, which they meticulously follow — because a good system ALWAYS produces results through painstaking hard work, focus and commitment.

Let's be clear here what I mean by a result. A result is a Yes or a No. That Yes could be anything from a commitment to a follow-up meeting right through to a large billable invoice. A no means you can park the sales opportunity and move on, giving you more time to focus on the next yes. It's the "don't knows" that suck up all your energy and kids you into believing your sales pipeline is richer than it is.

But don't be put off by a No. No stands for **N**ext **O**pportunity — it's a prelude to a Yes. The very nature of sales means you will get noes. If you only get yesses, sales would be easy, I wouldn't be writing this book, and we would all be mega-rich through the commission we've earned.

The difficulty for many business people is the lack of understanding about why they have had a No, which causes disappointment, anxiety and frustration. In many cases they may then opt out of selling altogether. This makes it very easy to then point the finger at successful salespeople and suggest they are successful because they are in some way dishonest.

This is not the case. I promise you that there is a universal sales system, and it works — every time. Providing you follow it. Whether you are a one-person business or a national account director for a large organisation or anything in between, this sales system will work for you.

So welcome to Sellology, and its three constituent parts:

- The Physiology of Selling, also known as words, music and dance;
- The Psychology of Selling, which covers Business Style Awareness;
- PROCES, our six-step sales system, which will help you improve your sales performance and ensure you are selling to your customer's needs, putting your meetings on their agenda, and always generating value whatever the outcome.

To perform this system well, you have to be honest with both yourself and your customer. Most importantly, you have to recognise that everything you do is for your customer, so the sales system needs to be clear and provide real value, as well as uphold your integrity.

People buy from people they like, get on with and trust. And people trust people who have others' interests at heart, not just their own.

I asked my associates at Kennedy Ross another question (we do talk a lot): How many companies have an embedded sales process containing indicators measuring the effectiveness of their sales system? Their answer was a resounding 'None'.

In my view, because the speed of technological change has outpaced the evolution of sales, we must facilitate the needs of the customer with a reliable, measurable sales system underpinned with honesty, respect and integrity. Or we will fail.

The sales system PROCES is straightforward to follow and mirrors the psychology we experience when making a decision to buy or use a service — something we refer to as Customer Transition.

Sales is about truth, and success in sales comes from sustainability. The world we live in gets smaller by the day and unscrupulous sales behaviour will always come back to haunt you sooner or later. PROCES will help you build your own bespoke methodology. It will work for both you and your customer by focusing on your customer's agenda, and it is designed to establish integrity, which will create value and sustainability.

What makes me such an expert?

At this point you may be asking, 'Why should I listen to you?' Good question. Over the next few paragraphs I will explain why. And if you are not convinced, I will refund you the cost of the book.

In a nutshell, I've been party to and overseen:

- Ten award-winning years with UK Telephone Directories Thomson (Yellow) Pages, completing every role from front-line telesales to national sales manager.
- A five-fold increase in turnover from £2.7 million to £14.3 million in three years as a regional manager with BT.
- A period of record-breaking growth as the sales director for UK and Ireland for 118118media.
- A return to profit, in under a year, for the *Manchester Evening News* as a commercial director of the Guardian Media Group, following five consecutive years of losses.

So what, you may be thinking.

Okay, well furthermore, during six years as managing director of Kennedy Ross Consulting Limited, I have worked with every conceivable size and type of business, including sole trader engineering businesses, small- to medium-sized businesses with teams of between five and ten sales people, and large multi-national corporates with sophisticated and complex sales teams. During that period, each and every one of them saw significant and lasting growth by using Sellology and our six-step sales system PROCES.

But what does this mean to you, the reader? It means that the Sellogy sales system will save you — save you from embarrassment, discomfort, exposure, bankruptcy, disappointment and failure. All of which can easily happen when your sales have failed.

Convinced? Hopefully you're now ready to read on rather than contact me about a refund.

By the way, science wasn't my best subject at school, languages were my preferred choice. So for all you fellow non-scientists, you can stop worrying about any scientific references in this book, there are none. Having said that, science, technology, engineering and maths (STEM)-based sales teams have thoroughly enjoyed working with Sellology and PROCES because of the systematic approach. Let me re-iterate. This is all about simplifying the science of selling, not complicating it. I am a salesperson first and foremost and proud to be one.

How to use this book

First of all you need to understand the importance of communicating clearly and succinctly so that your sales message lands with the required impact to the person you are selling to. This is explained in the chapter following this introduction, The Physiology of Sales, aka Words, Music and Dance

Then comes the chapter which explains the importance of getting off on the right foot when talking to prospective customers. The chapter includes the Business Style Awareness profiling tool, which you must complete as this will give you real insight into the business style you adopt at the start of your sales meetings.

From there, every chapter will explain each step of the six-step PROCES sales system, and illustrate:

- Insight into the sales behaviour.
- Overview of the behaviour.
- The Story, detailing real businesses and the real names of individuals as this is the only way I believe we can truly demonstrate the efficacy of Sellology.
- The Pain the business was enduring as a result of getting it wrong.
- The Fix we recommended and how it was implemented.
- The Value of that fix in pounds, shillings and pence, and the morale and motivation of the people involved.
- A hybrid of a checklist and a summary of the Fix at the end of each chapter titled "Line Up Your ...", as

in line up your ducks in a row. You will then be able to immediately and successfully introduce the newly learnt sales skills to your next meeting or call.

Why a system?

Everything done well in life has a system, a process. You may be saying to yourself, I'm not a salesperson. That may be true. However, if you have a system that covers all your selling concerns, and then apply it, those concerns will be removed. That's what systems do, they remove your bias, as in barriers to entry, and help you work through your obstacles, enabling you to be successful.

Sellology is a system you can work through to break down those emotional barriers to selling successfully. I can't change the way you feel about selling, but I believe I can change the way you think about selling — and that's the first step to a successful plan of action.

PROCES will empower you to diagnose where you are going wrong when a prospective customer tells you No, and empower you to maximise each and every sales opportunity to improve the likelihood of getting a Yes. It will safeguard you against silly actions and behaviours and secure greater sales success. High Five!

This system is based on decades of award-winning sales experience. It is a combination of the methodologies of the very best salespeople brought together in one easy to use system.

Customer Transition

Customer transition is the phrase best used to describe the psychological journey our customers make when deciding to buy. In other words, it reflects the psychological steps when making a purchase.

Sellology is built around the six-step sales system PROCES, which is designed to facilitate this journey by mirroring these psychological steps.

By using PROCES either as an end to end sales system or by using each of the behaviours in isolation, you will be able to identify where your customer is on their psychological journey and match those thoughts and feelings with the correct element (sales behaviour) of PROCES. It is important you understand this.

There are two illustrations to help you on pages 26-27. The first illustration maps out my thoughts as I go about purchasing a pair of trainers, the simplest of purchases. Each step I take is specific and remains the same.

Sometimes these steps may take a long time to complete, other times it's a snap decision. See if you agree if this is what you do when you make a purchase.

PROCES takes these steps and converts them into independent actions and behaviours which, when delivered, facilitate the transition (the thinking) of your customer from their initial interest to the actual purchase.

This leads us to the second illustration, which explains the customer's reactions when the Sellology behaviours of PROCES are implemented. The bubbles that sit alongside PROCES in the second illustration are the outputs which happen when the selling behaviours of PROCES are practised, and explain how your customer is feeling at that point. For example, the correct implementation of Obtain will generate the following two outputs: firstly, I will have identified the needs and gaps of my client; secondly, based on that analysis, the client has agreed that action is required to fill those needs and gaps. Implementing the actions and behaviours of PROCES engages your clients while facilitating customer transition.

PROCES & Customer Transition
This selling system is based on the steps we take whilst making the simplest of purchases

Plan	I've decided I would like some new running shoes so I research where is best (in my mind for the moment) and make a decision as to where to go. **So P stands for Plan**
Reach	I arrive in Manchester city centre, walk along the high street and see the sports shop, with lots of offers reaching out to me. When I walk in a shop an assistant walks up to me and also reaches out to me by asking: "Can I help you at all?" **R stands for Reach**
Obtain	I explain that I'm here to buy some new trainers and, over a period of a few minutes, the shop assistant asks me a few questions and obtains from me information about the type of trainers, the brand, the use, the price bracket etc.... I then agree (in my mind) that I would like to buy a pair of trainers today and commit to trying them on. **So O stands for Obtain**
Connect	I try some trainers on, different pairs, each time understanding how the trainer will benefit me, connecting the trainers with my needs and demand. **So C stands for Connect**
Elaborate	However, I'm still not convinced, so the shop assistant elaborates and explains further how the trainers I'm considering will fulfil my needs. To illustrate this he tells me third-party story of how this particular type of trainer helped many runners, especially those wanting to run longer distances. Exactly what I needed to hear. **So E stands for Elaborate**
Secure	The trainers are chosen, I like them and they seem fit for purpose. At this point the shop assistant says "Would you like me to put them behind the counter?", securing the next steps of this sale. To which I reply "Why, yes". **So S stands for Secure**

PROCES Facilitating Customer Transition

Each step can be used either to link to the next step or in isolation, depending on the business style of your customer. Get it right and both approaches will:

Guarantee a result (Yes/No)

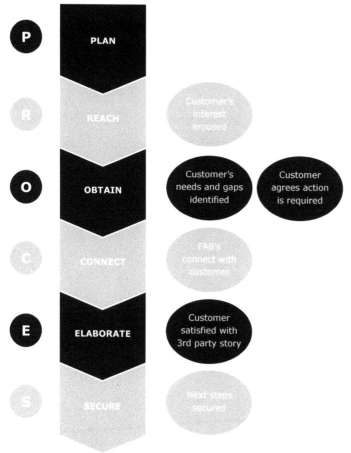

RESULT   The bubbles demonstrate how the customer needs to feel after each successful step of PROCES.

So now you understand the origins of Sellology and how it has been designed to "simplify the science of selling", providing you with a simple, powerful and repeatable system to increase your sales fast.

The PROCES selling system works by implementing the correct behaviours at the correct and most opportune moments when engaging with your clients, which I shall go into more detail throughout the book.

We will now move to the first part of Sellology the Physiology of Sales, aka Words, Music and Dance and why it is so important to ensure your communication is clear and concise whilst selling.

PART ONE

The Physiology of Selling: Words, Music and Dance

Clear communication is critical for your selling success

Communicating clearly

Albert Mehrabian, Professor Emeritus of Psychology at UCLA, is best known for his publications on the importance of verbal and non-verbal communications. He and his colleagues sought to understand the relative impact of facial expressions and spoken words in human communication. The physiology of sales in Sellology is built on his work, and the first of the three components that make Sellology. It specifically centres on the concept of Words, Music and Dance, and what happens when the words said (words) don't match the tone heard (music) and the body language seen (dance).

Mehrabian's research found that for effective and meaningful communication, these three elements need to support each other. In other words, they have to be aligned, make sense, be non-conflicting. This guarantees the message is received clearly with all three components (words, music and dance) working as one.

Here's a short example, for which I hope my wife will forgive me.

One afternoon I promised to work on the garden, as the lawn looked a mess. Then my neighbour asked if I wanted to go and watch Manchester United instead. (For the record I am a life-long Preston North End fan. However, when I weighed up the choice — garden vs Old Trafford — the decision wasn't a difficult one.) I thought I had better square it with my wife, so I asked her how she felt about the change in plans.

I said, 'Hello, my love, how do you feel about me watching the football today and doing the garden tomorrow instead?'

My wife replied, 'Fine.'

Her words, music and dance were at odds. Her tone (music) was edgy and sounded serious, her (dance) was upright, arms folded whilst glaring, and even though she said, 'Fine', she actually meant anything but fine.

Albert Mehrabian established that when words, music and dance are misaligned, or in conflict, as in the example I gave a moment ago, the recipient (me) receives the message in the following proportions:

- 7% Words
- 38% Music
- 55% Dance

This doesn't mean that the words are only worth 7%, it's just that in the presence of conflicting communication the words barely register. In my case, my attention was drawn to my wife's Music (her tone) and Dance (her body language). I barely heard the word 'Fine', yet I knew it wasn't fine.

Mehrabian's research illustrates that this level of conflicting communication occurs far more frequently than we care to imagine, and in my view is especially the case when selling. Mehrabian further concluded that when we don't have and can't see the Dance (the body language), the Music (the tone) increases to 93% of how the message is received. In this case (for instance, when speaking on the telephone), it's more important than ever that your music (tone) resonates with your customer so that your sales message lands correctly.

To complete a successful sale, it is critical for you to get your head around the words, music and dance concept if you are to get the most out of the PROCES sales system.

As I take you through each of the key PROCES behaviours you will receive direction on the recommended words, music and dance to ensure a successful interaction with your potential customer.

Here is another example, this time involving selling yourself. I was recently working closely with a sales director whose management team said they felt they could never quite satisfy him. Consequently, I observed the sales director in action. I saw him approach one of his sales managers with a file in his hand, glare at him, then in a serious voice — without smiling or pleasantries — calmly say, 'That's the best report you've done in months.'

The exchange left the manager wondering what the director's agenda was, and left the director wondering just what he needed to do 'to please these bloody people'. Quite simply, his words, music and dance were in conflict, causing a disconnection, and lack of clarity. Instead, the interaction should have been what we like to call at Kennedy Ross a high-five moment.

Now let's move on to Business Style Awareness, component two of Sellology, where you can profile your own business style when selling. You will finally understand why you get on with certain people in business and not others — and what you can do to get through those difficult and uncomfortable moments at the start of your sales meetings.
Enjoy.

PART TWO

The Psychology of Selling: Business Style Awareness

People listen to people they like — and
do business with people they trust.

Overview

Kennedy Ross works with a huge variety of businesses, and, regardless of their size, the question I am most often asked is, 'Why do I keep coming across people who don't like me when I'm trying to sell to them?'

Here's my answer...

Everyone operates within his or her own natural business style. It is enormously beneficial to recognise the four distinct styles (illustrated over the page) and decide which fits your approach most closely.

Simply put, you will get on best with the business style that's most like yours, and will have difficulty with the style that's least like yours. It is also true that all sales professionals are not made in exactly the same way, but I would go further and say that it is often the differences in our behaviours that can truly determine the great from the good.

To illustrate this, I would like to tell you a story of a fresh-faced young sales executive beginning to make his way in the industry, aeons ago, way back in 1990.

Our rookie was just starting out with Thomson Yellow Pages aka The Thomson Local Directory. After three months he returned to the HQ to complete the final part of his initial training programme and was almost certain he was going to be the top rookie in the business as he had been making more sales than any of the others he had started his career there with.

However, when the training manager put the league table up on the wall he was shocked to find that he was only in mid-table mediocrity.

When our rookie approached the training manager to find out why he wasn't at the top of the table, he was told that although his sales figures were huge, so were his cancellation rates. And his cancellation rates were what was killing his result. Oh dear.

That rookie was, of course, me. At this point the idea of style awareness was introduced. You see, while I was excellent at understanding the clients' needs and enthusiastically selling the benefits, getting the prospects excited and closing the deals, I was literally packing my briefcase and moving on to my next client before the ink was dry, leaving some clients feeling pushed and without any real connection to me or to the service.

I learned that some clients were happy with just the details of our offer and didn't want a relationship, whereas others needed me to spend a little more time with them so that they felt secure enough to trust me and Thomson and that the deal we had just made was in their best interests not just mine.

Business Style Awareness helps me identify the best way to share information and spend time with my prospects and help them feel secure enough to complete their purchase with confidence.

Business Style Awareness helps sales professionals gain a clear understanding of their "selling personality" and the "buyer personality" of their clients.

We live in oversupplied times. There are many other businesses selling similar products and services that compete with us for the same customers. Once upon a time the power lay with the sellers but now, with all the choice available, the power resides firmly with the buyer. Being spoilt for choice, buyers can take their pick and choose who they buy from, and in general most people only buy from sellers they like or get on with. Think about this just for a moment: have you ever bought something from someone you didn't like?

So, my simple rule of thumb for continued sales success is that if you want to sell as much as possible, you will need to find a way to get on with everyone you are selling to.

According to *Forbes* magazine, most people decide whether they like you or not within the first seven seconds of meeting you. The moment that person sees you, his or her brain makes thousands of computations, creating instant judgements about:

- Are you a person I can work with and potentially trust?
- Are you competent?
- Are you likable?
- Confident?
- Do we share any common ground?
- ... amongst many others.

These computations are made at lightning speed using tiny clues and impressions. This creates a problem for the salesperson: if you get off on the wrong foot it can make it significantly more difficult to get what you want out of the meeting or conversation. The technique I use to ensure I always get off on the right foot is called Business Style Awareness — component number two of Sellology.

Business Style Awareness equips us with the tools to ensure that the first seven seconds will be a success. The principles of Business Style Awareness underpins all of the PROCES sales system.

Business Style Awareness plays such an important role in the successful delivery of the PROCES sales system that I'm going to share with you our valuable profiling tool. This tool will help you understand:

- Your selling style.
- Your nemesis style, i.e. the style of the person to whom you will have the most difficulty selling.
- The changes in your actions and behaviour necessary to ensure you get the most out of selling to every style.

Overleaf, I'd like you to answer 25 multiple choice questions that will reveal your business style. All you have to do is choose the word that you think describes you best. To get the best out of the test, answer the questions openly and honestly, and purely in the context of business.

The first answer that pops into your mind is usually the right one, so move through the questionnaire as swiftly as you can. Complete the questionnaire before moving on to the next section.

N.B. If you would prefer not to mark the pages, the test is available to take on our website landing page www.kennedyross.co.uk You can take the test, get your results, then rejoin the book at page 49. It's your call.

1. Your least concern is for:	8. You tend to be:
• Routine • Causing change • People • Caution in relationships	• Impulsive • Direct • Encouraging • Hesitant
2. You most desire:	**9. You tend to be:**
• To control • To relate to others • To get involved • To organise	• Criticising • Driver • Conforming • Calculating
3. Your personal time frame is:	**10. You tend to be:**
• This week • Next year • Past years • Right now	• Determined • Hard–working • Tactile • Sociable
4. Your task completion is:	**11. You tend to be:**
• Delayed • Timely • Cautious • Immediate	• Judgemental • Indecisive • Harsh • Persuasive
5. Your greatest concern is for:	**12. You tend to be:**
• Feelings & relationships • Conclusions & actions • Principles & thinking • Dreams & intuition	• Dominating • Reacting • Methodical • Dependent
6. You tend to:	**13. You tend to be:**
• Reject conflict • Reject inaction • Reject involvement • Reject isolation	• Demanding • Persistent • Respectful • Inspiring
7. You are most oriented to:	
• Others • Intuition • Action • Analysing	

Business style

questionnaire

14. You tend to be:

- Enthusiastic
- Authoritative
- Precise
- Willing

15. You tend to be:

- Self-assured
- Dramatic
- Dependable
- Vigilant

16. You tend to be:

- Outgoing
- Orderly
- Efficient
- Agreeable

17. You tend to be:

- Adaptable
- Undisciplined
- Strong-willed
- Stuffy

18. You tend to be:

- Cautious
- Retiring
- Competitive
- Excitable

19. You tend to be:

- Visionary
- Caring
- Reserved
- Serious

20. You tend to be:

- Accommodating
- Secretive
- Aloof
- Opinionated

21. You tend to be:

- Dynamic
- Thorough
- Independent
- Helpful

22. You tend to be:

- Bold
- Gentle
- Humorous
- Perfectionist

23. You tend to be:

- Boisterous
- Relentless
- Obedient
- Rigid

24. You tend to be:

- Relaxed
- Disciplined
- Expressive
- Factual

25. You tend to be:

- Insensitive
- Impatient
- Self – absorbed
- Calming

Business style questionnaire (2)

	Doer (Pragmatist)	Actor (Player)
1	Least concerned with caution in relationships	Least concerned with routine
2	Control	Get involved
3	Right now	Next year
4	Immediate	Timely
5	Conclusions and actions	Dreams and intuitions
6	Rejects inaction	Rejects isolation
7	Action	Intuition
8	Direct	Impulsive
9	Driver	Calculating
10	Determined	Sociable
11	Harsh	Persuasive
12	Dominating	Reacting
13	Demanding	Inspiring
14	Authoriative	Enthusiastic
15	Self-assured	Dramatic
16	Efficient	Outgoing
17	Strong-willed	Undisciplined
18	Competitive	Excitable
19	Serious	Visionary
20	Secretive	Opinionated
21	Independent	Dynamic
22	Bold	Humerous
23	Relentless	Boisterous
24	Disciplined	Expressive
25	Impatient	Self-absorbed

46

	Friend (Companion)	Thinker (Analyst)
1	Least concerned with causing change	Least concerned with people
2	Relate to others	Organise
3	This week	Past years
4	Cautious	Delayed
5	Feelings and relationships	Principles and thinking
6	Rejects conflict	Rejects involvement
7	Others	Analysing
8	Encouraging	Hesitant
9	Conforming	Criticising
10	Tactile	Hard-working
11	Indecisive	Judgemental
12	Dependent	Methodical
13	Respectful	Persistant
14	Willing	Precise
15	Dependable	Vigilant
16	Agreeable	Orderly
17	Adaptable	Stuffy
18	Retiring	Cautious
19	Caring	Reserved
20	Accommodating	Aloof
21	Helpful	Thorough
22	Gentle	Perfectionist
23	Obedient	Rigid
24	Relaxed	Factual
25	Calming	Insensitive

Now multiply each column where you have circled your answers by 4, to give you a percentage score, then shade your percentage scores into the table.

	Doer Pragmatist	Actor Player	Friend Companion	Thinker Analyst
100				
95				
90				
85				
80				
75				
70				
65				
60				
55				
50				
45				
40				
35				
30				
25				
20				
15				
10				
5				

My primary personal style:
My secondary style:

The 4 Business Styles

Now that you have discovered your preferred selling style, let me summarise each of the four styles on the questionnaire. Hopefully you will recognise yourself!

The Doer (aka The Pragmatist)

- *Words* – efficient, authoritative, unfeeling, impatient, dislikes small talk, takes risks based on facts
- *Music* – tone of voice varies, fast-paced, tell style, confident
- *Dance* – controlled and/or limited body language, leans forward, strong eye contact, firm hand-shake, shows impatience

The Actor (aka The Player)

- *Words* – sociable, imaginative, competitive, tells rather than asks, takes risks based on opinions
- *Music* – varies widely in volume, expressive, speaks quickly, animated, raises voice to emphasise points
- *Dance* – considerable body movement, leans forward, smiles, expressive, holds constant eye contact

The Friend (aka The Companion)

- *Words* – calming, encouraging, soft-heartened, asks rather than tells, accommodating
- *Music* – friendly, warm, casual, emotion in voice, slow-paced
- *Dance* – slow gentle movements, open, relaxed posture, tends to lean back, little eye contact

The Thinker (aka The Analyst)

- *Words* – logical, analytical, data-oriented, avoid risk, asks rather than tells
- *Music* – slower-paced, moderate tone, little emotion in voice
- *Dance* – controlled, still or limited, tends to lean back but not in a relaxed manner, occasional eye contact, closed posture

When I describe the business styles it's important to recognise that in any list of characteristics the terms used are relative and not absolute, so beware of exceptions to the rule.

Also, just because a Doer is characterised as logical does not mean that they are always correct and neither does it mean that they are never illogical. It does mean, however, that a Doer is inclined to rely on a logical process when thinking their decisions through. On the other hand Actors rely on experience and how it has formulated their opinions and thinking. Both styles can be as wrong and as right each other.

In all cases of Business Style Awareness, the style characteristics are not necessarily good or bad. It's just the way people behave when they are in business.

In the case of the Doer, it means their emotionless approach helps them get the best in a given situation. Likewise, Actors' emotional approach works best for them.

To prove that both styles believe they are always right but can be clearly wrong, here is an example I recently came across whilst working in Blackpool, a seaside resort on the northwest coast of England.

A national account manager and I attended a meeting with a client to renew a large account. On arrival at 11.30 a.m. we were taken upstairs into an enormous office, with spectacular views overlooking the Irish Sea. The office was warm, comfy and inviting. The walls were decorated with awards the business had won; there were even certificates showing awards the business had been nominated for but had not won.

The client gave us a big, warm smile and exclaimed that he could predict — having lived in Blackpool all his life and from reading the clouds that were rolling in from the sea — that it was going to rain by 4 p.m. that afternoon.

The client's swanky office strewn with awards, the warm welcome, his tell style, and most of all his strong opinion on the future of the notoriously fickle English weather told me that he was an Actor.

The reaction of the account manager was to open a weather app on his iPhone and explain that it was not going to rain until later that evening. The Actor laughed, and said, 'You can't trust those things, they're never right. I'm telling you it will be raining by 4 p.m.'

Before the account manager responded I calmly agreed with the client and asked him to explain why he thought it would rain. The account manager and I listened to his explanation for 20 minutes after which we asked further questions to demonstrate we were interested, safeguarding the start of the meeting with good use of the Business Style Awareness behaviours. The meeting concluded and all objectives of the meeting achieved.

The question I have for you, the reader, is: who was right and who was wrong in their views about the impending rain?

There are two answers to this question. The first answer is neither — both could be right and both could be wrong. I don't know about you but I have seen the weather on my iPhone state it's raining when it's glorious sunshine outside my door. I can argue and say it's factual because the iPhone weather app states it and be completely wrong.

This is what I mean when I say a Doer (like me) can have the facts and believe they are right when in fact they are wrong.

The second answer and the most important one is that the client was right because at the start of sales meetings the client is always right, especially in the case of Actors. As salespeople we must recognise the style quickly, and then work towards, mould, shape and get on with our clients so that the first seven seconds of the meeting are a success. Remember, people only buy from people they know, like and trust, hence why the client was right.

Did it rain that afternoon or evening? No, it was a glorious week of weather and never a spot of rain in sight.

You should now be able to quickly recognise your nemesis style. For example, a Doer may well say, 'I've only got two minutes.' However, a Friend enjoys small talk and wants to build a dialogue. If the Friend is selling to the Doer, the Friend could attempt to engage in small talk (their natural style), despite having been told by the Doer he has only two minutes to spare. If this happens, it is very likely that the Doer will switch off. The Doer is then likely to become unresponsive, which in turn offends the Friend — effectively, two people setting off on the wrong foot. Therefore the knack in Business Style Awareness is to recognise your nemesis style quickly (ideally within seven seconds), and adapt your style accordingly. Just to be clear, you're not changing who you are as a person, you are simply changing your style to accommodate your client.

Here are a few more Business Style Awareness tips. The Actor and the Friend both respond from the heart, the Doer and the Thinker respond with their heads. So if I'm an Actor selling to a Thinker, I will completely rub the Thinker up the wrong way if I keep using phrases such as: 'In my opinion.' The Thinker doesn't want to know the opinion of the Actor — certainly not at the start of the meeting. The Thinker wants facts and figures, information from reliable sources to make an informed decision. If the Actor doesn't respond accordingly, the Thinker will switch off.

Interaction of Styles

Usually there is no natural clash between vertical and horizontal neighbours, such as:

- Thinker and Friend
- Thinker and Doer
- Doer and Actor
- Actor and Friend

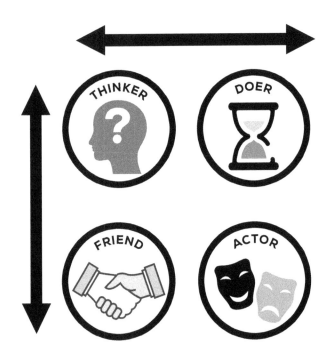

However, diagonal confrontations are likely to be explosive and counter-productive, unless one of the individuals adjusts their style.

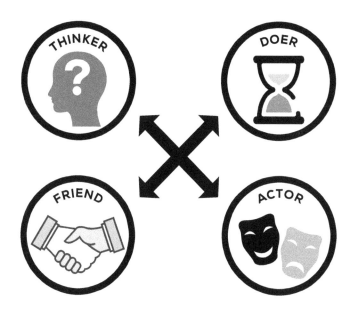

So there you have it. You now understand why you sell better to some people compared to others.

The PROCES sales system works with any business, any industry and any sales situation, providing you consider the impact of your communication (words, music and dance) and the business style of the individual to whom you are selling. Quite simply, you are who you are, and the same can be said for your customer. These are facts not judgements. If your business style does not complement the customer's style in any way, one of you has to adjust your style to get the most out of the situation. Since you are selling and the customer is buying, you need to be the one to alter your style.

The Story

SAL Abrasives (SA) is the largest independent manufacturer of abrasive technologies in the UK. When I began working with the company there was a mature sales team in both age and accounts. Consequently the MD promoted one individual from the internal telesales team with the specific objective of bringing in new accounts. His name: Lee Tootell.

Lee had a great first year with SAL Abrasives (SA), tapping into a market where new products and keen prices went down a storm. Lee's success came from enormous enthusiasm, lots of energy and an excellent work ethic, which included a lot of cold call activity and long days. He also collaborated with SA's suppliers, leveraging opportunities based on their relationships as well as SA's.

After completing the Business Style Awareness profiling tool he came out as a big Friend, which reflected Lee's love of small talk, and how he got on well with most people. The results proved that Lee was a naturally friendly guy. He focused his sales activity on cold calling on average 10 businesses a day in his amiable style which, I must say, works well when cold calling for new business. Think about it. A nice friendly chap cold calls your business, has the best products and services within your market place that money can buy. Why wouldn't you speak to him? He won every quarterly award and the annual award for outstanding sales performance. Every time he walked into the office it was high fives all round.

The Pain

Fast forward to the start of the next sales cycle and it was now time for Lee to renew his accounts, the largest of which was valued at £64,000, a significant sum to the company. Naturally he was cautious about calling this account but he had a cracking relationship with the buying authority. However, when he made the call he was horrified to find the buying authority had changed — his contact had moved on. Not only was there a new person making buying decisions, but their business style had also changed from what had been a big Friend to, in his words, 'an intolerant and impatient individual'. Also known as a Doer.

Now of course the new buying authority wasn't an intolerant and impatient individual at all, it was his Doer business style that seemed that way to Lee, a classic Friend. Despite the initial disconnect, Lee arranged a meeting and invited me to come along for support and to assess his performance. His objective was to introduce an annual increase in the price of the goods to the client of between 2% and 5%.

Prior to the meeting, Lee planned his approach carefully. On arrival he was greeted by the customer who immediately played the favourite Doer card, and said, 'I've got two minutes so you'd better be quick.'
Lee replied, 'How was your weekend? Let's get the kettle on...' the exact comments not to make to a busy Doer at the start of a meeting.

The client glared at Lee, and raised his voice. 'Did you not hear me? In fact, leave the paperwork there!'

'Er... I need to explain the rate increase. It won't take too long,' said Lee.

But to the Doer, Lee sounded weaker than ever.

'What part of "I only have two minutes" do you not understand? You'll have to come back.'

He turned to his secretary, and said, 'Bobby, get over here and show this chap out.'

Much to Lee's dismay, the client quickly left the room.

Lee and I returned to the car. He was white as a ghost. This was his biggest account. As anyone (including me) who has been in this situation will tell you, when your biggest account tells you to "do one" you get one hell of a stomach-wrenching feeling.

The Fix

Lee and I practised our next meeting before returning to the client. We agreed there would be no small talk, as Doers don't like small talk. We were going to stick to the facts and figures — in this case 3% was the minimum increase we could settle for — ideally we wanted 5%. We would then give the client the information he wanted, quickly and clearly (the music) with our heads held high and strong eye contact (the dance). Once done, we would calmly wait for his response. Now that we had planned and prepared for the meeting, Lee was more confident because he had his words, music and dance ready, and a strategy on how to deal with the dreaded Doer's rate increase.

On arrival, Lee approached the Doer, looked him right in the eye, gave him a firm handshake, and said, 'I am here to tell you what the rate increase is and agree how we move forward. How long do you have?'

The Doer said, 'Two minutes!'

Lee maintained constant eye contact.

'Having reviewed your account with my directors, we have agreed to offer you 3%, the absolute minimum rate increase of any of the customers at SAL Abrasives. What do you think?'

The Doer counteroffered: '2%.'

Lee looked him right in the eye. '3% is all I am allowed to give. Yes or no?'

The Doer paused for a moment, looked at Lee, smiled and said, 'Lee, that's fine, we will go with 3%. Would you like a cup of tea?'

They then had a chat as though they had been friends for the previous 10 years. High Five.

The Value of the Fix

The account renewed and went on to spend over £100,000 that year. Lee mastered his nemesis style and is still the top salesperson today.

You see, just because it is apparent that someone is a Doer in the first seven seconds of the call, doesn't mean they are not nice friendly people. It just means that they prefer to move through things quickly and factually. Any dithering and the Doer loses confidence in you, in this case a Friend, and that means potential loss of business.

You will notice when we start to talk about reaching out to customers that social media plays an important part in helping you contact potential opportunities. When I completed my first Style Awareness assessment in 1990 there were not many Friend styles to be seen. Now when my clients complete the updated Business Style Awareness assessments, Friend is the predominant style. I believe it's because of social media. We are now naturally friendlier human beings, there is an increased transparency in our lives and it makes sense to want to get on with everybody.

However, what I've also noticed is that business owners, decision-makers and senior managers more often than not are Actors and Doers. If a Friend calls a Doer and isn't prepared for the fast-talking straight responses, the Friend may be offended, hence my comment at the start of this chapter and the question I am most often asked: 'Why do I keep coming across people who don't like me?'

Line up your Business Style
Awareness

- People decide whether they like you or not within 7 seconds of meeting you.

- There are four business styles: Doer, Actor, Thinker, Friend. You need to understand the words, music and dance required to facilitate the needs of your nemesis style.

- DOER When selling to a Friend, don't forget the small talk.

- FRIEND When selling to a Doer, you will be pressed for time so don't initially engage in small talk — have your facts ready.

- ACTOR When selling to a Thinker, have your facts and figures prepared for analysis and resist the temptation to talk in opinions.

- THINKER When selling to an actor, speed up your sale and be warmer, more personable.

PART THREE
P is for PLAN in the Kennedy Ross sales **P**ROCES

Proper planning and preparation prevents piss-poor performance.

Overview

Over the years, sales planning has been an enigma to me. To plan or not to plan, that is the question. I say that because on the one hand very smart, quick-thinking, fast-talking sales people will say they either don't need to or haven't got time to plan. On the other hand, having implemented different planning methods throughout the years, I am conscious of the danger of wasting time. I've seen sales managers insist on levels of planning which far outweigh the potential benefits, demoralising the salesperson who then loses all motivation for planning at all.

Despite that, planning is more important and more beneficial than ever before. Planning today is about having as warm a connection as you can possibly muster, so you can give yourself the best opportunity to sell to your prospect. Cold is bad; warm is good. In other words, and a lot of which will be highlighted in the Reach chapter, there's never an occasion when you can't find out something about someone and their business. The important information on everything and everyone is often in the public domain. So there's no need to ever go into a prospect cold when there is so much warmth to be gained by good planning.

The Plan chapter is divided into two sections – external planning and internal planning. External planning is where we research our potential customer using social media, industry intelligence and competitive information. Internal planning is where we consider how we will apply the PROCES sales system to your sales meetings, in particular in the areas where you feel less confident and/or less informed.

What I'm saying here is that straightforward planning works every time, while over-planning can be a waste of time. Clarity creates opportunity.

The Story

Centurus is an award-winning Lancashire-based business that deals with educational establishments on a national basis, in international student-related services. With a distinct focus on technological solutions, Centurus develops revolutionary systems and services to assist institutions streamline student recruitment and manage international students.

Dawood Fard, the company's MD, approached Kennedy Ross for some business planning support. He had spent extensive time planning and researching the systems by which overseas students apply to university, and found that many universities were wasting time, resources and money processing these applications. This was compounded by the fact that a lot of overseas student applications were being completed by so-called agents, who claimed they could ease the system and in some cases get the student into their chosen university.

This activity was accepted by the universities who claimed that it helped match students' needs to university requirements. The problem was that all these agents and universities were using multiple software packages to submit the applications, which accounted for the wasted resources.

Centurus's solution to the universities' problem was a single point of contact that would streamline the application process for international students applying to UK educational establishments.

The Pain

Dawood chose the universities he felt would be interested to see him, then worked with his sales director to make appointments with the people he thought most appropriate. On one occasion he drove all the way to Plymouth from Preston, only to find that the person he made the appointment with wasn't even in the department of international student applications. Needless to say, the wasted 280-mile drive gave him valuable opportunity to consider his approach, while his sales director gently wiped the tears from her eyes.

In summary
- Miles travelled: 560
- Cost of travel: £120
- Hours travelled: 12
- Hours planning the presentation: 6
- Sales: £0.00
- Loss of face: Priceless

One thing you can say about Dawood and his team, is that they have bounce-backability. Determined to continue selling his software solution, Dawood and his team worked with me to improve his planning, take advantage of his opportunities, get more sales and ensure he didn't waste any more time.

The Fix

This is what we did... Firstly we established which universities had the highest number of overseas applications, information that was freely available on the internet. Then we drew up a target list of the top 40 education establishments. We researched information from the websites of all 40 colleges and universities to discover the departments that were responsible for international student applications. We then identified the contacts and decision-makers in each of the departments.

At this point we gathered a lot of valuable information about those key decision-makers. We reviewed their profiles, which may prove crucial when identifying their preferred business style. For example, if the LinkedIn and Facebook profiles were littered with awards and achievements and lots of personal information, it would indicate this person was likely to make decisions from the heart, and is an Actor or Friend. Alternatively, if the LinkedIn and Facebook profiles have limited information with fewer pictures, thoughts and feelings, this could indicate a Thinker or Doer.

It is important to understand at this point in the research that these are just considerations. This is the

Plan part of PROCES and we haven't actually spoken to the client yet, merely assimilated information in the public domain. We also added competitor research to the mix, which can be split into two important questions. We asked: How does Centurus stand out against its competition? What will be the impact of using Centurus on the client university's competition (i.e. other educational establishments). In other words, what will be the university's competitive advantage that Centurus will bring to the table.

As you can see, a methodical approach to external planning can quickly build valuable data before approaching the potential client. Having identified our potential opportunities based on industry research, company research and social media research, and understanding the competitive marketplace, we then moved onto the internal planning steps.

We did this by reviewing the remaining steps of PROCES to understand which elements may be challenging in the face-to-face meeting. In other words, being prepared so that Dawood would deliver his A game, even when the client might pitch a curve ball.

This can be illustrated below. But before you read on, let me explain that you are about to read how PROCES is planned without actually knowing what PROCES can do. With that in mind, may I just say, Read on, you'll get it. As I said, it's about Simplifying the Science of Selling, and of course you have those chapters ahead of you.

Reach

In this case, the chosen method of Reach was to make an appointment over the telephone. This involved designing a script for appointment making with Dawood and then practicing the delivery of the script. Particular focus was given around the words and the music as this is a phone call!

Obtain

- Dawood carefully prepared and practised his preamble — and his magic question for when he will be face to face with his potential customer.
- He also prepared three open questions as back-up.
- He then rehearsed his desired outcomes so that he could drive the wedge and deliver the summary and commitment.

Connect

In advance of the appointment making phone call we prepared three FABs (Feature Advantage Benefit) and one BAF (Benefit Advantage Feature), which is more appropriate when dealing with Doers. Dawood also practised his words, music and dance to build his confidence and ensure a quality delivery of his FABs in the forthcoming meeting.

It will help you to know here that Dawood came out as an Actor in the Business Style Awareness profiling tool — his nemesis style is that of a Thinker. This meant that one of Dawood's FABs had to have real detail in it — data and sources of data — so that he was prepared for the worst case (nemesis style) scenario.

Elaborate

Anyone who has met Dawood will tell you that he is a very good storyteller. Consequently, elaborating in the meeting by telling a third-party business-related story of how he had successfully solved another university's overseas application problems, meant that he could Tell it like Tarantino, a concept I shall explain later.

Secure

For this stage we decided to create a one-page document which would be used as a "leave behind", a piece of information that enables the decision-maker to easily communicate to their colleagues why the university should invest in the Centurus software. Secure is the final stage of PROCES in which we Secure the next steps of the sale. Dawood also agreed he would control the follow-up, in other words, keep the next steps of the meeting firmly under his control, not the client's. Both these actions make certain Secure has been completed conclusively.

Once the planning was complete, Dawood and his sales director looked forward to their next visit — another long drive away, but this time armed, or rather planned, to the teeth!

The Value of the Fix

One big advantage about the meeting being such a long drive was that it gave Dawood and his sales director the opportunity to practise their Connect behaviours, the FABs, and their Elaborate behaviours — Tell it like Tarantino through third party business-related stories — to near perfection.

The meeting at the university ran smoother than expected and Dawood acknowledged that this was due to having a good Plan. The result was an agreement with the client to purchase the Centurus software. High Five.

The PROCES sales system, combined with Dawood's focus on the Plan and his marvellous software invention, has since resulted in Centurus becoming a national award-winning organisation.

Summary

The external planning process — industry research, company research and competitive research — has to be completed before you can move to the internal planning process. This information will help shape your thinking around the questions to ask and FABs to deliver.

The internal planning process is about being able to identify where you are potentially weak in the PROCES sales system and what you must do throughout the steps of Plan to make sure you are prepared for any eventuality, and that you bring your A game to the meeting.

Most of all, don't plan just for the sake of it. Instead, make your planning specific and relevant to the areas you are most concerned about and want to excel in.

Line up your Plan

External Planning

- Target prospects using social media
- Facebook
- LinkedIn
- Company website
- Industry research
- Google search
- Company research
- Companies House
- Competitor research
- Google using your key search terms
- Identify and agree challenges based on the above

... then you can move on to ...

Internal Planning

- **Reach** — Decide on the most effective method of reaching your prospect.
- **Obtain** — Your preamble and the magic question need to be relevant and precise.

- Prepare 3 to 5 relevant open questions.

- Understand how you will take your clients' information, drive the wedge and turn that into an agreed need for which you have the solution, via your summary and commitment.

- **Connect** — Plan to deliver your FABs with conviction, focusing on your words, music and dance and always have a BAF up your sleeve if you struggle selling to Doers.

- **Elaborate** — Be prepared to Tell it Like Tarantino when you deliver your third party business-related story — once again, your Words, Music and Dance must be at the forefront of your mind.

- **Secure** — Do you understand what is required for you to leave the meeting in the best possible controlled way so that the next steps are in your hands not theirs?

R is for REACH in the Kennedy Ross sales

PROCES

Check the prevailing winds of business and tack accordingly.

Overview

The way in which we, as salespeople, Reach out to our customers has changed dramatically over the last 15 years. Previously, other than writing a letter, we had two options, namely, cold calling in person or telephoning. Both methods had the same objective in mind, to get in front of the P.A.N. — the individual who has the Pounds, the Authority to make a decision, and the Need to buy or use your service.

I mentioned earlier that during the years of selling in the Land of Milk Honey, aka between 2003 and 2007, it became all too easy to send an e-mail and hope for the best. We were going through an economic boom, demand was growing, supply was static and we had these new and improved methods of technological communication, which meant it was harder to fail and getting lucky became much more commonplace when reaching out to potential customers. Then gradually as the recession of 2008 began to bite, instead of refining sales systems, businesses relied on the same old systems to produce the same results, and hoped for the best.

Well, the only hopes I know are Bob Hope and No Hope. Hope is relying on luck. The sales system PROCES ensures that you create your own luck by following a renowned and proven sales system. By the way, the days of picking up the Thomson's Yellow Pages and starting your telephone calls at letter A and fishing at Z are long behind us. As discussed in the Plan chapter: cold is bad; warm is good. There are many new, sure-fire ways of producing target opportunities where you can establish some form of warm connection.

For this chapter I have listed a summarised view for each of the Reach methods, then related the real life business story in which I focus on the most difficult way of reaching out to your customers: cold calling by telephone. The final part of this chapter delivers top tips on Reach enabling you to implement your preferred method immediately.

Social Media

> 'Social Media means you never have to
> do business with a stranger ever again.'
> *Neil Simpson, Kennedy Ross*

Social media has become one of the top forms of communicating with people you have never met, when you want to progress your opportunities.

Twitter

Twitter is often misused by businesses. It is very good for "social listening" to key groups of clients and data mining current trends and market issues using hashtags. Twitter Ads (paid posts) can greatly increase the chance of being seen by your chosen audience. In 2015 Twitter made available their own analytics system to help users assess and monitor the effectiveness of the messages they share.

LinkedIn

LinkedIn is great for creating prospects and then leads using the Groups and Advanced Search functions for researching and then contacting individuals and companies. LinkedIn also has its own analytics system and method of paying to promote posts and updates to increase market reach for content created by businesses.

Facebook

The narrative style of Facebook can help you understand not only the personalities and Business Style Awareness of the individuals you are looking to meet, but also the key values of their business.

Once a Page (as opposed to a personal profile) has been set up, it is possible to create Boosted Post and Facebook Adverts to directly promote to specific audiences.

Once a page acquires 30 Likes, a substantial range of analytical tools are unlocked to increase the targeting of messages and engagement with intended audiences.

Instagram

If one of your potential clients is on Instagram you will be able to quickly identify what kind of company they are and what kind of Business Style Awareness they are exhibiting.

YouTube

A super versatile platform that can be used at almost every point in the customer journey, from marketing and prospecting for customers, to customer service and product "Bedding In" and configuration. Think about it as having your own business's television channel.

Also, YouTube has the world's second largest search engine and tends to be the search engine of choice for the under 25s (it's owned by Google).

In addition to the available native analytic systems on each of these platforms, there are a number of specialist tools to help you get the best out of social media marketing and sales in terms of audience targeting, scheduling posts and creating useful content.

Digital Marketing

E-mail marketing

There is a saying amongst digital marketers that "The money is in your list" — your email list. Careful management of your email list with a structured offer can yield a consistent stream of both new and recurring sales. I strongly recommend using a specialist e-mail partner like Mailchimp, AWeber, Infusionsoft or similar, to get the best out of managing your list and increase sales.

SEO (Search Engine Optimisation)

This process can be thought of as the new shop window. By ensuring that your web pages are optimised for search, you can increase your chances of climbing the rankings and appearing on the first pages of Google, Bing and other search engines.

PPC (Pay Per Click)

PPC is best described as a form of micro-advertising online. It's like having a private road that carries your ideal customers right to your shop window.

Business Networking

The new cold calling, done face to face at organised business events rather than knocking on doors.

Traditional Methods to Reach Customers

Cold Calling

The old call calling, on the phone or out in the field (which still results in you getting very wet in inclement weather) can also be effective when required.

Making Telephone Appointments

The method of Reach that causes the most pain and on which I get the most comments around how difficult it is. I will use this method as the story.

The Story

Thomas Moss Fruit and Veg is a wholesale distributor and supplier. Their target market includes cafés, restaurants, nursing homes, takeaways, sandwich shops and hotels. As a result of a sales strategy review, I was asked to help Thomas Moss recruit a dynamic sales individual. And by a dynamic individual I mean a hunter versus a farmer.

Hunters are what I describe as "new business predators"— they are keen to hunt out new opportunities and have a propensity to close in for the kill, or rather the sale, quickly.

Farmers are typically relationship builders who enjoy spending time laying the groundwork for the future, sowing the seeds of long-term relationships and cultivating business. All of which can be described as practices of good account management.

Tony Morawski, the managing director, had an objective

to double the turnover of one of his business channels within three years. He planned to achieve this primarily through increasing those channels' new business revenues — hunting. The new business hunter's strategy was to increase business via two routes.

The first route was through cold calling smaller businesses – the café shops, takeaways, etc. — and close these on the day, whenever possible. The other route was through much larger opportunities; these opportunities had to be connected via LinkedIn and then called on the phone to make an appointment. A meeting would then be arranged where the hunter's objective would be to get the larger business on board.

Dave is an Actor and a hunter-type salesperson. This means he is friendly, outgoing, competitive, and has strong opinions. As mentioned previously, one of the most important aspects of cold calling is making sure your prospects are as warm as possible — warm is good. In this case, Dave had previously worked with an insurance company who was a supplier to Thomas Moss, and on request very kindly produced a list of businesses they dealt with. We analysed the list and, based on the Thomas Moss business proposition, turned it into 20 high-value opportunities with whom Dave connected on LinkedIn.

The Pain

Dave then decided to make the appointments. They didn't work out too well. The reason for this was that Dave was making the appointments the same way he closed his business in a face-to-face meeting. There was was no real structure to his appointment making — he didn't establish any key criteria, and relied largely on his personality. In the first six attempts he did not make one appointment.

The impact on the business wasn't that great at that point because we had not lost anything except some potential opportunities. However, the impact on Dave was considerable. It affected his confidence, morale, belief and dynamic attitude and approach, to the point where he decided telephone appointment making was not worth his while, contrary to the MD's growth strategy of bringing in larger and higher value accounts.

The Fix

Dave and I worked together to create a script. Before I go into the script, let me explain its purpose. Quite often I come across objections from sales people when I propose scripts, based on the fact that reading a script over the phone sounds staged and "sales-y". My view, based on my experience of many well-executed scripts, is that they do sound staged if you don't bother to practise and learn them. I believe it takes 14 attempts before it doesn't sound like a script. My message has always been the same: when it comes to scripts, practise it before delivering it. It amazes me that people think they can get a result without having a system and then practising that system. All of the cold calling telephone scripts I use contain the following five critical elements. Provided these are included in your script, you won't go wrong — you may get noes but you won't go wrong.

1   Introduction

The introduction must always mention yourself, your company, and the name of the person you wish to speak to. You must always state that 'it is a quick call' or if you have got through to the PAN, always ask, 'Do you have a moment to speak?', all in one sentence and wait for the answer.

2   FAB (Features, Advantages & Benefits)

This is your opportunity to connect with your customer in an impressive way. This is not about bragging, but rather establishing common grounds of credibility.

3   Value Statement

Tell the customer what value you will bring to their life if they engage with you.

4   Go for the appointment

Offer alternative times and dates and confirm the appointment.

5   Consolidate your appointment

Ask if they would like an e-mail confirming the appointment. Explain that you may text the day before the appointment and then double-check that the person you are seeing is the PAN.

... and as for the script, it went like this:

Introduction

'Good morning, it's Dave Woods calling from Thomas Moss Fruit and Veg. It's only a quick call, do you have a moment to speak?'

FAB

Thanks for connecting with me on LinkedIn. We provide hotels like yours with the widest range of prepped veg [Feature] so your chefs can save valuable time [Advantage] which means more importantly you will save money while improving the quality of the food you serve to your residents [Benefit].'

Value Statement

'I'm in the area visiting hotels understanding who they currently work with on their fresh produce supplies and explaining how Thomas Moss Fruit and Veg can benefit their business.'

Go for the appointment

'What I would like to do is arrange a brief meeting whilst I am in the area to review your fresh produce supply, understanding any challenges you're currently facing and most of all explaining how we can support you in the delivery of your food services. Which is better for you, Wednesday afternoon or Thursday morning?' [Negotiate time and date]

Consolidate your appointment

'Just to confirm, it is yourself who makes any decisions on produce spend? [Consolidate] I'll be with you at 4 p.m. on Wednesday afternoon, and as mentioned, what I will be doing is understanding what your current situation is with your fresh produce and if we establish some common ground, suggest some recommendations on how we go forwards. Is that okay?'

There are a couple of caveats you will need to consider...

Business Style Awareness

Make sure you pick up on the business style of the individual you're selling to, remembering which business style you are and your nemesis business style. In this case, as an Actor, Dave naturally struggles with the Thinker. And who could be potentially holding the purse strings at these large hotels? Finance directors, typically Thinkers.

What Dave did to plan for the tricky Thinkers was to make sure that his FABs contained detail, for example, how long Tom Moss had been established, current large customers, delivery schedules, etc., because this is what the Thinker needs to know to make a decision.

Gatekeepers

Gatekeepers are there to stop their bosses from having their time wasted and support them to be productive. If you explain with the same words and the same tone to the gatekeeper as you would to the owner or the PAN, you will more often then not be put through. It is the lack of clarity in the initial engagement with the gatekeeper, combined with a misguided approach towards them, that often turns the gatekeeper against the caller.

At this point Dave and I practised his words, music and dance, remembering that because Dave is on the phone, there is no Dance, or body language, to support his sales message. This means his Music (tone) will now constitute 93% of how the message is received (if delivered poorly) by the potential customer. Consequently, his tone has a massive influence on the success of the phone call.

After Dave and I practised — in particular practised around his nemesis Thinker style — Dave began making some phone calls to prospective clients for an appointment. I listened in. The first two calls did not go well. The reason was that he didn't stick to delivering step one, the Introduction, without interruption.
So we practised again and again and again.

Then Dave made a really good, solid appointment with the 2nd biggest hotel in the resort town of Lytham St Annes. The hotel's finance director was a Thinker, and by delivering step 1 without interruption Dave went on to deliver points 2 – 5 and made a successful appointment.

Well done Dave – High Five!!

The Value of the fix

On average, an appointment made with a larger business successfully closed for Thomas Moss is worth 12 times more than the average cold-call door to door sale that Dave brings in. He was able to secure his largest contract to date — £6,000 a month of goods sold, —earn great commission and, most importantly, cement the Reach part of PROCES as standard working practice. Oh, he was also very pleased with himself.

Line up your Reach

- Plan ahead to ensure your prospects are as warm as possible

- When making appointments, build a script based on the guidelines described and practise it in a safe environment until it doesn't sound like a script.

- Keep Business Style Awareness in the forefront of your mind as this will influence your Music, i.e. tone.

- Get a result, a yes or a no. And in my book, an appointment making conversion rate of 1 in 4 is a good outcome to begin with for potential new opportunities.

Top Tips on Reaching Out

Twitter

As mentioned, Twitter's best used for listening and researching trends, business sectors and client groups. In order to narrow down the amount of information visible in your Twitter feed you can create groups of customers, prospects, business leaders or competitors into specific lists. Be positively selective about who you connect with, in other words the connections need to reflect the company you're pursuing or represent the values you hold.

Choose your Tweets very carefully, consider your ideal client, and only share information that provides value to them. Like and re-Tweet the best Tweets of the people/ organisations you want to connect with. Critically, have a view point — remember, your followers will create impressions of you and your business depending on what you are liking and re-Tweeting.

LinkedIn

Research the companies you want to connect with — and the key people within these companies — by looking for common connections, interests, skills or workplace history. Make contact via an inbox message or invite —

quickly establish your credibility during this unsolicited contact by referring to your connection as mentioned above, then... get to the point quickly by giving them a FAB about you and your business.

Initially the goal is to get a 1st level connection acceptance, which gives you 2nd level access to the connections they have. Once you've secured your 1st level connection, you can make a follow-up approach. Thank them for the connect and begin a relevant conversation.

Facebook

Facebook Pages can be very useful for top-of-funnel activity. By which I mean it is very easy and cheap to reach out to accurately targeted audiences via the Boosted Post and Facebook adverts.

Facebook can be used to tell the story of the experience of your customers, and is great for two-way conversations with your customers, whether that be via an open or closed group helping to co-design new products or embed new products into existing organisations.

Business Style Awareness can be identified by reviewing

Facebook profiles, so this really helps when you are reaching out to new customers.

Instagram

Great for showing the more visual side of your business, helping to make the buying steps more personal (people buy from people, and most of all those that they know and trust). You can use it to show your products and services in use by your existing customers. Currently it does not use an algorithm like Edgerank, the Facebook tool that decides who sees what. On Instagram, every post is shown to every follower, every time. You can search using hashtags to research trends, markets and customer groups.

Digital Marketing

To get the most out of your digital marketing campaign in order to Reach your target market, I strongly recommend you utilise the services of a professional in each of the respective areas. They are very different disciplines and should be treated as such. When you do hire a professional, make sure you are clear on your objectives and proposed budget. Determine your measurable return on investment criteria — number of leads, contacts made, opportunities, e-mails opened, pages landed on, appointments generated and — most of all — sales made!

Business Networking

Create a 30-second elevator pitch using the FAB approach and practise your words, music and dance. A well-rehearsed elevator pitch will ensure you Connect with your audience quickly.

The cornerstone of your networking activities should be the people with whom you have already done business: colleagues, customers and suppliers. Invest time in these important relationships. Meet up with them and find out if there is anything you can do to support them, and request referrals in return.

Develop network advocates who will go out of their way to recommend your goods and services without being asked or expecting anything in return. Take time to develop the relationships with key members of your network.

Follow up your new contacts and opportunities within 48 hours.

Cold Calling

Look smart and professional, clean (shiny) shoes,

appropriate business dress. Be planned and prepared, have your business cards at the ready and introduce yourself with confidence. You will also need to ask for permission to take a few minutes of their time before continuing. If you don't get permission, it will impact your confidence and the way in which you deliver your next piece of information may well be rushed and unclear, preventing you from pursuing your opportunity successfully.

Face to face cold calling is where I recommend you flip your FAB into a BAF, as discussed in the Connect chapter. This will immediately inform your potential customer how you and your business will benefit them. It will also buy you a little more time, which is always nice to have in these pressurised circumstances.

Business Style Awareness can work wonders here. For example, if you were to walk into a new business displaying awards, trophies and certificates of success, the likelihood is you are about to speak to an Actor. Alternatively, files and books stacked high and wide suggest you are about to deal with a Thinker. An uncluttered, tidy and organised environment would be that of a Doer; finally, photographs of the family and pets, with tea and biscuits readily available tells you that you may be about to deal with a Friend.

Cold calling epitomises the phrase, "A No is a prelude to a Yes." So be prepared for the No and stay true to your objectives about why you are cold calling.

O is for Obtain in the Kennedy Ross sales PROCES

The most difficult job when selling to your client isn't to find the right answer, it's to ask the right question.

Overview

I'm a naturally nosy individual. I ask a lot of questions because I want to know what's going on. Asking the right questions in the right way is the hardest part of any sales system because it combines open questions with closed questions. Then you have to somehow capture the information you've received by memorising and summarising the conversation, finally committing your potential customer to agreed actions. All of which has to be completed while utilising Business Style Awareness.

Phew, and before you decide to skip this chapter, let me assure you that, as with the rest of this undertaking, you will soon be able to implement Obtain as effectively as any other part of PROCES.

There is an accepted rule when it comes to the balance of listening and talking in a sales meeting. In the first half of the meeting the salesperson should be talking for 20% of the time and listening for 80%. In the second half of the meeting this is reversed, 80% talking and 20% listening.

Done well, you will be viewed by your prospect as engaging, friendly and most of all consultative in your approach. Done poorly, you'll be viewed as a pushy, narrow-minded salesperson. And none of us want to feel like that. Let's face it, salespeople are renowned for talking too much, whereas effective use of the Obtain behaviours will ensure that customers and clients don't feel as though they have been sold to. Get ready for some useful direction on how to question potential clients and get the answers you need to sell your products and services with real confidence and empathy.

I believe relevant questions engender good decisions. The better the questions I ask my potential customer, the clearer their answer will be. And the clearer their answer, the easier it is for me to sell accurately and concisely. First, let me explain the difference between open and closed questions.

An open question is one that generates answers other than Yes/No/Don't know, and leads to opportunities to engage with clients in an open and consultative manner. This approach encourages conversation and helps identify issues, allowing the questioner to summarise and commit the conversation to present their business solution to their clients' challenges. Open questions enable you to expand on a customer's issue, or as I like to call it "drive the wedge".

I keep six honest serving-men
(They taught me all I knew);
Their names are What and Why and When
And How and Where and Who
(Rudyard Kipling, The Elephant's Child, 1902)

Open questions always begin with Who, What, Where, Why, When and How, plus one more that Kipling didn't mention: Which.

Of course, the bigger and more time-sensitive your customer's problem, the more likely you can fit your solution to their needs sooner rather than later. The deeper you drive the wedge by asking open questions, the quicker the client will require the solution. By comparison, closed questions encourage one-word answers and often curtail the dialogue, creating awkward situations. This doesn't mean you never ask closed questions. The skill in questioning clients is to only ask a closed question when you know the answer, or if you are looking to complete a particular line of questioning so you can move on to another. Is that clear? Well don't worry, here's a good example involving a solicitor in court questioning a man on trial for drunk and disorderly behaviour.

Solicitor (S): 'Where were you on the night of 12th December?'
Accused (A): 'I was walking along Leicester Square.'
S: 'Who were you with?'
A: 'My mates.'
S: 'Why were you there?'
A: 'I was celebrating my pal's birthday.'
S: 'How did you celebrate?'
A: 'I had a few beers.'
S: 'How many beers did you have?'
A: 'About 10 pints.'
S: 'How did you feel?'
A: 'A little giddy.'
S: 'How were you walking?'
A: 'Unsteady.'
S: 'What did your eyes look like?'
A: 'Glazed.'
S: 'How was your speech?'
A: 'Slurred.'
S: 'Is it safe to say you were drunk?' (Closed question)
A: 'Yes, indeed I was.'

All the questions, with the exception of the last, were open. The closed question enabled the solicitor to complete his line of questioning. He established what he needed and then moved on to his next line of questioning, which will again be led by open questions. Yes, I know the example is a little tongue-in-cheek, but when applied to sales meetings the principle is exactly the same. If you want to ensure an excellent rapport with your clients, while exploring their issues so that you can offer your solution quickly, keep your questions open until you are as sure as you can be of the answer to the closed question.

Obtain in the PROCES sales system can be defined as follows:
- Rapport build
- The magic question
- Drive the wedge

The Story

FISC Healthcare is a market-leading national distributor of products and related services to the healthcare industry, i.e. nursing and care homes. They pride themselves on partnering with their clients to provide solutions that continually improve the culture and the quality of their clients' care homes. This care exceeds expectations, which means FISC clients increase profitability through improved occupancy and staff retention.

They are a very dynamic organisation. Shortly before my association with them they had completed an excellent rebranding that introduced a new approach to what they do, centered around honouring dignity in care. Their sales team was very down to earth, enthusiastic and committed to the FISC brand. Eddie Fishwick, the managing director, contacted Kennedy Ross and we introduced the PROCES selling system.

The Pain

Their challenge was how do they disturb the complacency of their competitors' customers, increase their number of clients, and continue the great growth they had enjoyed in previous years. After working with the team in the field it became clear that they needed particular help around the Obtain part of PROCES — asking the correct questions that will provide information against which they could successfully sell.

Neil Burwood was a relatively new account manager to the business and handled himself well. He was smart, enthusiastic (an Actor in style) and willing to learn. We both attended a meeting with the manager of a care home, who Neil had already identified by phone as a Doer. It was likely that she would claim to be pushed for time, require facts and figures and remain poker-faced at the start of the meeting, all of which had the potential to unsettle Neil if he had not planned and prepared his questions well enough.

My recommendation to Neil was to write his questions down. As an Actor, Neil felt that he could ask the questions without writing them down. I explained that despite the number of years I've been selling, I still write my questions down. In the end he agreed to write down the magic question, *but not the open questions.*

...so what is the magic question?

This is a question that, when asked correctly, will 100% guarantee a clear and honest answer. Before we ask the magic question we have to ask for permission to ask it. But that can only be done once you have built rapport.

...so what is building rapport?

That's the pleasant chit-chat we all engage in when we first meet our customers. Its length depends on the style of the person you're talking to: longer with a Friend, shorter with a Doer.

Let's assume you have built rapport, with cups of tea in hand and everyone sitting comfortably. Then we move to the second part of the magic question, where we ask for permission to ask the question. Technically, this is a rhetorical question because you know what the answer will be — it will always be Yes.

One of the ways in which you ask the question is as follows:
'Thanks for the tea, Tracey. You may have had time to think about the meeting since we last spoke on the phone, you may not have done, but [it doesn't matter if she has or has not] either way, and before we start the meeting, do you mind if I ask you a straightforward question?'

I must stress how important it is that you use these exact words:
'Do you mind if I ask you a straightforward question?'
...as opposed to:
'Do you mind if I ask you a question?'
'Do you mind if I ask you a quick question?'
'Do you mind if I ask you a personal question?'

... and so on, all of which may potentially allow different responses to the word 'straightforward'. Straightforward means no bells or whistles, no hidden meanings or connotations. By asking the question in this way, and in a way that mirrors the style of your client, you will, undoubtedly, receive a straightforward answer.

At this point my clients often ask me, 'What if they say No to the straightforward rhetorical question?' Quite simply, if positioned as described, a positive response is the only answer you'll receive. However, you may get a No from the likes of an Actor because they like to be in control. My advice here is, sit tight and smile — very quickly the Actor will give you the answer because it is all about them at this point.

So now you've asked for permission to ask the magic question — of course, they don't know it's the magic question — and they reply, 'Yes', 'Not at all', 'Go ahead', etc., you then ask, 'What would you like to get from this meeting over the next 20 minutes or so?'

Let's just break down the components of this question.
- It's an open question (because it begins with 'What')
- It's directed at the client
- It's asking for an outcome
- It lays down the potential length of the meeting

The most remarkable thing about this question is that

every single time you ask it — providing the steps are followed exactly — the answer is always something you can immediately work towards.

Again, in training, I'm asked, 'What if the customer gives you an answer you cannot deal with?' In Neil's case, we were there to discuss care home consumables, so he would expect an answer concerning those supplies. But I can assure you here that what will not happen is that the answer you receive will be off the wall, such as, 'Can you help me with the central heating, my boiler has packed in.'

Going back to our client's story...

Neil built rapport briefly, then asked for permission to ask the question: 'Since we last spoke, you may have had a chance to have a think about this meeting, you may not, either way, do you mind if I ask you a straightforward question before we start the meeting?'

The manager replied, 'Not at all.'

Neil then said, 'What would you like to get from this meeting over the next 20 minutes or so?'

He did this without referring to any notes, as he'd clearly memorised the steps.

The response he got was, 'Great question, Neil. I'd like to understand how you can guarantee that the delivery for certain consumables will be on time each week — and by the way, I don't have long.'

At this point, let me say well done to Neil for asking the magic question in the perfect way — High Five! Unbeknown to me Neil was completely thrown by the answer, in particular, the use of the word 'guarantee'. The care home manager continued with her curt approach (typical of a Doer), and said, 'Can you guarantee your deliveries Neil?'

Neil had not prepared his questions, and suddenly started asking closed questions.

'Do you want the pads delivery guaranteed?'

The manager replied, 'No.'

'Do you want things delivered earlier in the week?'

'No.'

Before we knew it, the Obtain part of the sales system was completed in two minutes flat, which isn't what we set out to do, and certainly didn't give us the information we needed to sell to her needs and requirements. I was able to recover the meeting by acting out a Columbo moment. (For younger readers, Columbo was a scruffy TV detective who always saved his best question once the meeting was over and he was exiting the room).

I said, 'Just one more thing...' and managed to ask the following questions.

'What is it that you want guaranteed delivery on?'

'When do you want it delivered by?'

'What would be the impact of your deliveries being late?'

'Who does this affect?'

'What will happen if nothing changes?'

'How soon would you like this fixed?'

We agreed the next steps, the manager was satisfied and the meeting ended. We set off for another appointment, with Neil giving himself a hard time about the fact that he hadn't asked open questions. I reminded him that he had positioned the magic question perfectly, and it was simply the fact that he had not written the questions down that caused him to panic under pressure. I also pointed out that it's easier for me as an observer to notice what is being said when not actually involved in the sales meeting itself. In all these cases, two minds are always better than one.

The Fix

Our next appointment was with another care home manager to whom Neil had spoken several times. Despite that, he was going to prepare the questions this time. On arrival, the woman greeted us, and we were just about to settle down in a comfy armchair with a nice cup of tea and two digestive biscuits when she introduced us to the company owner and his son, who had driven 150 miles especially for the meeting.

Neil and I looked at each other. You could clearly tell that the owner and his son were serious: emotionless and expressionless — a Thinker and a Doer, Neil's first and second nemesis styles. We were taken upstairs to an organised office that had a big pile of paperwork in the middle of the desk.

The owner, without looking at Neil, said, 'I'm not sure why you are here. What could you possibly have to offer?'
I quickly worked out he was a Thinker because his eye contact was, at best, limited, and he was asking questions at the start of the meeting.
His son added, 'You have two minutes.'
Most definitely a Doer.
Cue a very brief rapport build from Neil and a perfectly delivered magic question.
The owner stared at us for what seemed like an eternity (of course, he was thinking), then replied, 'We are building a large extension to our home and I would like to see how you can help.'
Neil was taken aback by the answer, but at that point was able to refer to his prepared questions while he gathered his thoughts.

He then did exactly what he should do in the Obtain part of PROCES.

He said, 'To be able to understand where I can help, I have some more questions I'd like to ask.'

He then asked a series of open questions:

'How many beds is this extension going to hold?'

'What equipment is required?'

'When will the work commence?'

'What is the patient profile?'

By asking those questions, Neil identified the one area for which they had no plans — suitable hoists for patients with serious back injuries. Neil then went on to complete the third part of Obtain, "driving the wedge".

So what's driving the wedge?

These are the questions we ask to unlock the emotional drivers of our client. Emotional drivers are the emotional elements of your client's issue which, when uncovered, will drive them to consider some form of action. So you need to ask questions that concern thoughts and feelings, designed to elicit an emotional response. Actors and Friends tend to be driven by emotional drivers more than Thinkers and Doers, yet all are affected by them in some way or another. Those who think from the heart, i.e. Actors and Friends, show it more than others.

The more you ask these questions the bigger the emotional driver and more apparent it becomes that action is required to fill the gap. Each question is about knocking in that wedge deeper and deeper so that the customer's issue becomes larger and wider. The need for required action develops more and more into something that is urgent, difficult to ignore, emotionally driven and requires immediate consideration. What was a crack in your client's business has now become a gaping hole because of your drive the wedge questions, and this hole requires filling before your client's business sinks and disappears. Well that's how it's supposed to go. I suppose my example is a little melodramatic, but if you don't get to your client's emotional drivers you will struggle to get agreement that a solution is required now rather than further down the line.

Let me introduce a couple of caveats here. Firstly, empathy: it is critical that you empathise with emotional issues otherwise you may come across as heartless, so lots of 'Oh reallys' and 'Oh dears' are required, in other words gentle acknowledgements that you understand how your client might be feeling at this point. Also, if you go in too hard, your client will switch off and see you not as an empathetic sales consultant but as the harbinger of doom. So, when asking drive the wedge questions don't overcook it and show you care.

In this case Neil had established that the client did not have suitable hoists for patients with serious back injuries. Neil then went on to drive the wedge. This made the issue go from a small crack in their plans to a gaping chasm — if nothing were to change, it would lead to a potential loss of business and face. By unlocking the client's emotional drivers, Neil's created a sense of urgency, thus:

'What would happen if this issue wasn't fixed'?

'How much business could they lose?'

'What would happen to the reputation of the business?'

'Who would they be letting down?'

'What would be the impact on his patients?'

'How did the client feel about this on-going problem?'

'What would be the impact to the business with all those empty beds?'

'When did he want the problem fixed?'

'Would he like Neil to help?' (Closed question.)

It was a great example of driving the wedge and making this both a painful and rewarding experience for his customer. Like the earlier example of the solicitor, Neil asked open questions until he wanted to close off a line of questioning, then he asked a closed question. The drive the wedge questions around feelings uncovered the emotional drivers and created the urgency and drive for the client to consider buying or using Neil's services sooner rather than later

Finally, Neil summarised the information he had gathered by repeating it back to the customer, then gained the client's commitment that they were in agreement with all the information discussed and what would happen next.

Neil said, 'What you are telling me is that you need a lift-hoist quoted for, so it can be included in the plans for the build. And you need this done ASAP, before it causes major issues to your business and potentially loses money. Getting these hoists will increase the reputability and the profitability of your business. Would you agree?'

The reason why you must always summarise and commit your Obtain is to make sure you have asked the right questions, listened carefully to the answers, and established common ground with your client. Only then can you move to any other part of PROCES.

If you don't summarise your conversation and gain commitment that you're both in agreement, you run the terrible risk of going down completely the wrong route and running into a big fat No at the end of your meeting.

In response to Neil's summary, the client smiled and told Neil he was absolutely spot-on with his assessment. Well done, Neil. High Five.

The Value of the Fix

We walked out of the meeting with an opportunity to produce a quote totalling £25,000. Four weeks later this quote turned into an order. Most of all, Neil now understands how important it is to write the questions down during the Obtain part of the sales PROCES, maximise every opportunity, and always remain on his client's agenda.

Prior to any meetings, Business Style Awareness must remain at the forefront of your mind. If the customer doesn't buy into you within the first seven seconds, it will be difficult for them to buy from you. You need to plan and be prepared (as per our planning chapter).

When using the Obtain behaviour, I strongly recommend you follow these three steps:

- Engage with your clients (rapport build)
- Establish where and when you can help (the magic question)
- Drive the wedge

Line up your Obtain

Step 1

- Build rapport based on your Business Style Awareness Assessment and ask for permission to ask the magic question as follows:

- 'You may have had time to think about this meeting since we last spoke, you may not; either way, do you mind if I ask you a straightforward question before we start the meeting?'

Step 2

- Ask the magic question exactly like this: 'What would you like to get from this conversation over the next 20 minutes or so?'

Step 3

- Plan three to five relevant open questions before the meeting.

- Remember that open questions start with who, what, where, when, why, how or which.

- Closed questions prompt Yes or No answers and help close off the line of questioning and gain commitment.

- Drive the wedge. Ask your client questions designed to uncover their emotional drivers. This will make them feel uncomfortable, so demonstrate empathy otherwise you will come a cross as heartless.

- Repeat back and summarise what you've heard to confirm you are both on the same page. You will now feel confident enough to move to the next part of PROCES.

C is for Connect in the Kennedy Ross sales PROCES

People have little interest in purchasing a bed; what they want is a good night's sleep. Features tell, benefits sell.

Overview

Following our Obtain, we are at the end of the first period of interaction during which your customer was talking for around 80% of the time. At this point (based on Customer Transition), your Obtain will have identified your customer's gaps and needs, and you and your prospective customer will have reached an agreement of the actions required to fill those gaps and needs.

It's fair to say that you are now at a point where your client, irrespective of their business style, is prepared to let you talk more fully and will listen to what you have to say. However, one of the most common mistakes in the world of selling is that some people have a tendency to throw out information about their product or service without tying that information to the essential needs of the client based on the information gathered in Obtain. Typically what I find is a tendency to "feature dump". This means talking about all the great things your product or service can do, without referring to the *benefits* your products and services will bring to your customer.

The phrase "features tell, benefits sell" means exactly what it says on the tin. If you are just pontificating about how great your services and products are, you are probably not connecting with your customer. Failure to Connect prevents the customer from appreciating the benefits of your solution. Why should they choose you as their preferred supplier if there is no connection? As soon as you start to personalise these features and convert them into benefits by explaining what they mean to your customer, you will begin to convince them that what you are offering is potentially the correct solution to their problem.

I have found the most effective way to do this is to utilise benefit statements, which explain why your product or service is the most effective means of solving their business problem. Specifically, benefit statements are powerful because:

- They are directed at your customer's needs and requirements and will resonate quickly with them.
- They connect the features of your business to the benefits of your client, which makes it

straightforward for them to understand and appreciate what's been said.

If you and your client are in agreement at this stage about the benefits your business can provide, you are well down the road to securing your sale.

I strongly recommend that you Connect with your customers using FAB statements. I know the acronym is a little cheesy, but I never said I wasn't going to be cheesy; this is a sales book after all. FABs provide a clear structure on how to deliver your features, advantages and benefits. Here's a short example:

- This is a bed (feature) F
- So you can lie on it (advantage) A
- Which means this bed will ensure you get a good night's sleep and you will feel nice and refreshed in the morning (benefit) B

I appreciate that it would be completely uninspiring if you were to deliver FAB in the way I've just described, but I have spelled it out because time and time again in my experience working with businesses, the Connect part of sales meetings is more often than not only about features. There is no mention of any advantages or benefits, which can lead to deferred decisions and no sales. More often than not it is followed by a whole heap of self-examination and personal disappointment in the failed attempt at selling.

The Story

Hammond Trotter is a Manchester-based solicitors' practice that specialises in defending people who have allegedly committed driving offences. The managing partner, Martin Hammond, approached me to improve their in-bound call conversion rate, which was standing at 10%.

The business worked in the following way: through clever marketing activities they would receive incoming phone calls from potential clients. Typically a driver would call and say that they were caught speeding, which could potentially mean they could lose their driving license. Martin Hammond and his solicitors would then attempt to convince the caller that they should use Hammond Trotter to defend them.

The Pain

Oh, if it were so simple and the phone call ended there. As with many marketplaces, this is a very competitive environment, with four or five key players vying for a limited number of opportunities.

The first thing I did with Martin's team was to introduce PROCES, and believe me that was met with some scepticism — mainly because the solicitors didn't know what they didn't know, if you see what I mean. We reviewed and discussed their Words, Music and Dance, an area in which the solicitors were strong. Their communication was clear and concise, and in particular their music (tone) was balanced and relevant. Next, we worked together on completing and understanding each solicitor's Business Style Awareness. In turn they quickly learned how to identify the business style of the callers.

As potential clients called in, the solicitors took them through the Obtain part of PROCES — the magic question, open and closed questions, driving the wedge, and summarising and committing the information they established to move through to Connect. Unfortunately, they didn't really convert many more enquiries — one or two maybe, but certainly nothing substantial. There was one call in particular during which a headmaster explained that he had been breathalysed, and through the clever implementation of Obtain, Martin Hammond established the potential for the headmaster to be found not guilty. As far as Martin was concerned, it made sense for the headmaster to go ahead and agree to use Hammond Trotter; instead, the headmaster said he wanted to speak to another firm to get more information. Needless to say he didn't come back and Martin lost the business, valued between £1,000 and £10,000.

Martin is a big Doer and this loss made him feel extremely disenchanted and he began questioning his investment in the training with me. You see, if somebody's going to buy something from you, once they've appreciated and agreed that they have a need that can be serviced by your business, they then have to understand what the benefit of your service is going to be to them. To help them decide they should buy, they need to Connect with you. What was missing from Martin's approach was the FAB of Hammond Trotter, which if delivered with the correct words, music and dance based on the business style of the caller, would satisfy their requirements. This would prevent the caller from trying someone else and positively impact Hammond Trotter's conversion rates and profitability.

The Fix

Martin, having missed this big opportunity, agreed with his solicitors that together we would design several FABs and then practise their delivery. Here are three examples of the FABs we created:

- F — We have over 25 years' experience.
- A — So we know what we are doing when it comes to defending drivers.
- B — Which means you can be assured I'm confident I can help your situation.

- F — One of our partners is the chairman of the Society of Motoring Law.
- A — So he is one of the top experts in motoring law.
- B — Which means he will provide you with the most up to date information on road traffic defences to help your case.

- F — We only deal with road traffic offences.
- A — So we are real experts in this field.
- B — Which means you will get the best representation money can buy and are more likely to find a way out of your predicament.

Now let's be realistic here. There are occasions when I insist my clients say the words exactly the way they are written (for example, the magic question). FABs are a bit different. If you were to say them exactly as they were initially written, there's a chance it could sound staged, sales-y, and nobody likes to be sold to, do they? The key, as with everything else we have spoken about in this book, is practise, which creates familiarity and breeds confidence.

By way of example, let's look at the first FAB. This became much more natural when delivered after a period of practise. We went further. An open question was introduced to the script to ease their way into delivering the script:
'What do you know about Hammond Trotter?'
And now the FAB.
'Let me tell you we have over 25 years' experience (F) and driving defences are our bag (A), so rest assured, I am confident I can help your situation (B).'

After much practising, the solicitors started taking the calls and utilising the FABs. Within two weeks the conversion rate had doubled to 20%. This delighted me. However, being the driven individual that he is, Martin wanted to improve his conversion rate still further. He felt that his solicitors were only delivering the FABs well to Thinkers and Friends. This wasn't a surprise as the Business Style Awareness profiling tool confirmed that they were all Thinkers and Friends.

I listened closer to the incoming calls, and it became clear that the callers who were Doers were preventing the solicitors from engaging early in the telephone conversation. This was because the Doers wanted to know what was in it for them up front, not after 5–10 minutes of rapport building and questioning. If the Doer didn't establish quickly what was in it for them, the telephone call became difficult and often ended in the caller deciding to look elsewhere.

I explained that there was a way of communicating FABs to Doers — by flipping the FAB into a BAF. In other words, deliver the benefit statement first. This will grab the Doer's attention and give the solicitor the time required to Obtain and then Connect with their potential client. Let me be clear, I only recommend you use a BAF when you need to get your message across quickly, which is always the case when you are dealing with Doers. Here are a few examples of phrases to lead in to benefit statements:

- 'You can be confident that...'
- 'You don't need to worry because...'
- 'You can be reassured that...'
- 'This will give you peace of mind because...'

So now let's take one of Hammond Trotter's FABs and turn it into a BAF:

- F — One of our partners is the chairman of the Society of Motoring Law.
- A — So he is one of the top experts in motoring law.

- B — Which means he will provide you with the most up to date information on road traffic defences to help your case.

... can be delivered thus:

- B — You can be confident we will provide you with the most up to date information on road traffic defences to help your case.
- A — As we have one of the top experts in motoring law.
- F — Our MD is the chairman of the Society of Motoring Law.

The Value of the Fix

The team's conversion rate soon saw more than a three-fold increase compared to their conversions before I worked with them. Martin's solicitors were now brimming with confidence, especially in the way they dealt with their nemesis style, the Doer, by delivering BAFs. Most of all, the ability of the whole team to communicate effectively how Hammond Trotter can benefit their clients expanded into face-to-face meetings, and even into court proceedings. High Five.

Please remember that the more relevant your FABs and

BAFs are, the more likely you will Connect with your client, and prevent them from considering your competition as an alternative. For your client to consider your business as the preferred solution there needs to be a connection.

Line up your Connect

- Design and agree 10 FABs around your products and services, then choose your favourite three.

- Practise your FAB delivery until you can say them with confidence.

- Consider the impact of your FABs on the various styles (Doer, Actor, Thinker, Friend).

- Pick a FAB and turn it into a BAF.

- Use the question, 'What do you know about [your business name]?' as you segue into the FABs.

E is for Elaborate in the Kennedy Ross sales
PROCES

If you're gonna tell a story, tell it like Tarantino

Overview

First of all, let me say that we can't pull together a sales system without talking about selling itself. So this is the part of PROCES that requires you to sell. We do this by telling a story. But not just any story. We have a saying at Kennedy Ross: "Tell it like Tarantino." And before you panic, for all you non-salespeople out there, it's just another part of the system — structured, supported and scripted, and, like all the other chapters, it's straightforward and easy to follow. So hold on tight, take a deep breath, and here we go.

Allow me to remind you where we are in our sales system journey. This is the part of customer transition where the buyer needs to have their buying criteria satisfied. This is the time for you to compellingly describe your competitive advantage. In other words, why should they buy from you? To answer that, you will need to Elaborate on what you've already said, that is, Tell it like Tarantino.

Quentin Tarantino is renowned for directing and producing films with compelling storylines. This makes them believable, they draw you in, and they prompt or prick your imagination, all of which makes his films very engaging, if you like that sort of thing. I do. Therefore, if you're going to tell a story — because this is what we're doing here, telling a story — then tell it like Tarantino.

The idea came from the film *Reservoir Dogs*, which is about a group of gangsters who commit a robbery that goes disastrously wrong. Within the group is an undercover policeman, played brilliantly by Tim Roth, who needs to convince the gangsters that he is a long time "hood". To do this he has to provide them with a plausible back story explaining how he had entered the crime world. His mentor, a senior policeman, gives him a story to learn. After a couple of days practising, Tim Roth meets his mentor again and delivers the story. But it wasn't believable, it wasn't real enough. His mentor explains that for these gangsters to believe his story they need to know who he was referring to, understand the background, recognise how it made Tim Roth feel, the sounds, the smells and the emotions he had at the time the story happened. The devil is in the detail, which will make the story believable and real. Only then will the gangsters trust him and accept him. Needless to say, he practised the story over and again, and lo and behold the gangsters believed him.

Please don't start thinking that sales is a life or death situation. However, unless you deliver your story with the necessary detail, you could actually end up dying on your feet. In other words, not winning the sale. So you, the seller, have to convince your client, the buyer, that it is your service / product which they should choose as the preferred solution to their need. This is effectively achieved by delivering a third-party business-related story in which you must convince your customer that based on existing customers' prior experiences, you can demonstrate that you have the credibility, background, experience and most of all the evidence to fix their problem in the way they want. You can offer your story in a casual, unimpressive, boring and meaningless way, or you can tell it with conviction, passion and detail, as Tarantino would.

If you want a prospect to buy or use your service you need to top their expectations and blow them away with your solution — without compromising your values.

The Story

NaanDanJain is the second largest provider of irrigation equipment in the world and their number one supplier in the UK is a company called Ripple Aquaplast. Managing director Stewart Penny approached me to help him increase his market share within the UK. The primary targets were soft fruit growers who were currently being supplied by their main competitor — and largest provider — Netafim.

To fully understand the story it is important to know how the irrigation system worked. The system consisted of lines of tubing strategically placed around a field, to which were attached drippers — small cylindrical feeders that controlled the flow of water. There was one significant difference between the Ripple Aquaplast system and that of their competitor, Netafim. The Netafim dripper cracked at −5 degrees; NaanDanJain's could withstand frost down to −20 degrees.

Stewart and his team identified where the key soft fruit growers were situated around the UK, then drew up a plan of attack.

The Pain

On one occasion, the team visited a client opportunity worth in excess of £250,000. Their potential customer was looking to upgrade their irrigation, but was happy to continue with the original Netafim system. To Stewart's credit, he had completed a very thorough Obtain part of PROCES during which he drove the wedge by establishing that in the severe winters of 2010 and 2011, the Netafim drippers had cracked when the temperatures fell as low as -14 degrees. The impact to Stewart's potential customer was:

- In excess of £100,000 loss of produce
- Six members of staff made redundant
- Two years running at a loss

All of which was down to the fact that the Netafim dripper could not withstand frost below -5 degrees. Despite Stewart's in-depth Obtain and confidently delivered Connect, the meeting was adjourned until further notice. There would be no change of supplier on this occasion. This was a kick in the teeth for Stewart and his business. They had the answer to the customer's problem, their product was better and more suitable, but unfortunately the potential client remained unconvinced.

The Fix

Stewart isn't a natural storyteller. He is a Doer: pragmatic, logical and straight talking. Therefore his stories have to be based on what he believes to be logical facts, otherwise he will not deliver the story with conviction, like Tarantino. I asked Stewart to consider what he believed was required for him to be able to tell his story with conviction. I explained that unless he went beyond his customers' expectations and blew them away with his solution he will not win the order. In other words, he needed to elaborate on what he had already discussed and tell it like Tarantino. This is what happened.

A couple of weeks later we were driving down to meet the client with Stewart practising his story over and over again, just as Tim Roth did in *Reservoir Dogs*. We also discussed Stewart's words, music and dance. We both knew the client was a big Doer, which meant Stewart's words needed to be succinct, clear and pragmatic; his music needed a strong tone and level pitch delivered at a good pace; and his dance had to be an upright stance while facing the client head on. We arrived at the meeting and Stewart began implementing PROCES. He initiated a brief rapport build with the client (appropriate as both are Doers), asked the magic question, then got an agreement with the client that if Stewart could provide a worthy explanation of why the client should switch suppliers, the client would switch.

This is what Stewart said: 'Let me tell you how NaanDanJain dripper will work for you. Last time we met, you mentioned that five years ago you installed Netafim drippers; three years ago that decision cost you thousands of pounds and six people their jobs. I don't want this to happen to you again. However, I needed to be 100% convinced that my system would never let you down. Therefore, since we last met I conducted an exercise of my own. I placed five NaanDanJain drippers and five of our competitor's drippers full of water in my freezer with the temperature set at minus 18 degrees. This is 4 degrees lower than any frost we have had in this region. After ten days, I removed the drippers from the freezer, allowed them to defrost and discovered the competitor's had cracked but NaanDanJain had remained intact. This is why I can sit here, look you straight in the eye and tell you with 100% confidence that if you re-order from your current supplier and we have another severe winter, you will be in exactly the same position you were in three years ago. Alternatively, if you order the NaanDanJain dripper, not only are you going to pay less, you are also going to save jobs and secure your future business. Can you see how the NaanDanJain dripper can work for you?'

While Stewart was telling this story, I noticed his body language was mirroring the client's. They were both sitting upright, straight-faced and emotionless, and the information Stewart was delivering was succinct and factual, which is exactly how you deliver a third-party story to a Doer.

The opening sentence of Stewart's third-party story statement — 'Let me tell you how the NaanDanJain dripper will work for you...' — was designed to get the client's attention. The final sentence — 'Can you see how the Nanjandane dripper can work for you?' — was all about gaining the commitment that he understood exactly what Stewart had just explained to him, and that he was in agreement about the solution. If you do not start and end your Elaborate with these two statements, the likelihood is your client won't listen and therefore will not commit to your solution.

The Value of the Fix

What can I say? The story worked. Stewart got the order — a very healthy £175,000-plus at the required margin, creating a win-win for both parties. High Five. I asked him afterwards how he felt telling the story even though he didn't see himself as a storyteller. He said that he still didn't see himself as a storyteller, but because he had prepared and practised his third-party business-related story, and most of all because he really did feel that his solution was the best for that situation, he was proud of the fact that he was able to tell it like Tarantino, exceed his customer's expectations and blow them away with his solution. In summary, when you Tell it Like Tarantino, the third-party business-related story has to be a solution, a true story and related to the customer's problem. It's the integrity of your story that gives you the confidence to Tell it Like Tarantino.

I'm often asked whether a story should be embellished when telling it like Tarantino. Here's my view: first, let's look at two definitions of the word embellishment:

- A decorative detail or feature added to something to make it more attractive.
- A detail, especially one that is untrue, added to a statement or story to make it more interesting.

This is why salespeople get a bad name. The first definition is acceptable (shortly I'll explain how Business Style Awareness will make your story more attractive). However, the second definition is out and out lying, and as I have mentioned and will continue to mention, integrity in sales is paramount and must never be substituted with half-truths and lies. So I am saying that, while occasionally there may be a smidgeon of embellishment, this is governed by and based on the business style of the person you are giving the story to. This will make the story more attractive and sit well with your customer because you will hit all the right notes.

Stewart was telling it like Tarantino to a Doer, so the information had to be clear, practical and factual.

If he had been telling the story to a Friend, he would have had to talk a lot more about the feelings of his customer and how his product could make the customer feel better.

If he was telling the story to a Thinker, the story would have had to include additional analysis, data and sources of the data for them to make a decision.

Finally, if he was using Elaborate to an Actor, the story would have had to include how it would make a big difference to his life, his business and his customers. Let me state unequivocally once more, PROCES must always be implemented with integrity, with your business values and ethics in the forefront of your mind, and with your customer's agenda as the number one driving force to a successful sale.

Line up your Elaborate

- Tell it like Tarantino.

- You are delivering a real/true story of one of your customers whose problems were solved by your solutions.

- The story must always contain

  - a time

  - a place

  - names

  - a backstory (i.e. the problem)

  - the impact of that problem

  - the steps taken to fix the problem with your solution

  - a happy ending.

- How do we deliver them? You need to start the story by saying, 'Let me tell you how [insert your business name here] can work for you.' Then once you have delivered your Elaborate, say, 'Can you see how [your business name] can work for you?'

- Wait for the answer. If the answer is No, understand why, then Elaborate again.

S is for Secure in the Kennedy Ross sales PROCES

Seven out of 10 pitches end without the salesperson asking for the order – of the three that do ask, two give up after the second refusal.

Overview

We go to extraordinary lengths to find prospective customers — we Plan our approach, Reach out to make an appointment, Connect by enthusiastically delivering our FABs. Then we Elaborate —Tell it like Tarantino — only to be told by the customer at the end of the meeting, 'Thanks for the information. I'll give you a call next week.'

It's a startling fact that around 70% of sales calls end with the salesperson failing to ask for the order. This is often due to fear of rejection, something I have witnessed far too often. Based on what I've seen over the last few years, over 90% of all written quote communications (delivered by letter, email or fax) do not control the follow-up. What I mean by this is that the quote is sent and then not followed up, either in a timely way or not at all.

There is a definition of the word Secure that epitomises how it fits into PROCES: "Succeed in obtaining something, especially with difficulty."

The Secure element of PROCES focuses on keeping the closing part of the sales call firmly in your hands. These three elements will help you achieve this:

1. Controlling the follow-up — the biggest issue and the simplest to fix.
2. Closing — tips of which are in the Top Tips on Closing section following this chapter.
3. How to negotiate — using the Kennedy Ross Negotiation Matrix (an easy way to work out the most favourable outcome while negotiating), also at the end of this chapter.

Closing, of course, isn't a dirty word, yet it is perceived as such. It's not helped by the likes of the actor Alec Baldwin in the brilliant (sales) film, based on the play *Glengarry Glen Ross*, throwing his Rolex watch into the middle of the boardroom table towards a group of dishevelled, disheartened and poor performing sales people, while shouting with mixed expletives: "ABC, Always Be Closing." No wonder closing terrifies the average businessperson and puts buyers off.

This chapter will outline exactly what Secure looks like. At the end there are also some further tips based around my favourite top 13 closing techniques and how to negotiate to create a win-win.

Closing the sale, as with all the skills in the sales system PROCES, can be learned in isolation, but that is not always enough to ensure you Secure the deal. If you position the magic question correctly and accurately, the answer you receive is your first step towards your close. The general view has been that closing happens at the end of a sale — I'm saying it's at the beginning, and runs throughout the sale.

First of all let's understand what your client means when they say No. This could mean:

- Not on the terms you describe
- Not at the moment
- Not in your timescale
- Not at that price
- Not from you
- Convince me further
- I'm getting interested but I need more information

Resistance from clients is perfectly normal and should be expected. Often the buyer is seeking reassurance that the decision is a good one. Salespeople who are Friends and Thinkers deal with these issues differently to Doers and Actors. For example, Friends and Thinkers may find asking for the order almost embarrassing because they haven't followed a robust sales system. They will do anything to avoid asking for the business for fear of rejection. They will extend the discussions, all the while delaying the inevitable, relying on hope — something I've already said that you should never rely on when selling. Actors and Doers may come across as aggressive — the "typical" salesperson — talking their customer to death, battering them into submission and inevitably losing the sale. The result? Lower prices, squeezed margins and demoralised salespeople.

The Story

Uretek has been providing subsidence and ground engineering services across the built environment for 35 years. They offer ground improvement stabilisation, re-leveling and void filling across major transport infrastructure, industrial and commercial facilities as well as residential properties.

I was invited into the business by the managing director, Roland Caldbeck, to help him increase sales. They employed around 10 engineers who travelled the country as "salespeople", visiting companies and private households with subsidence problems. They would complete a thorough assessment of the clients' needs

(Obtain), articulately communicate the FABs (Connect) of the business, and Told it like Tarantino in abundance (Elaborate) — then failed miserably on Secure. They didn't control the follow-up, they never attempted to close, and got nowhere near the realms of negotiation.

They were focused and committed to their roles. However, woe betide anyone who referred to them as salespeople. I did, and it resulted initially in alienating the team. They could not bear to be viewed as such, even though in my eyes that's exactly what they were. Having said that, I'm also aware that if people don't like me then they won't buy from me — whether that's my ideas, my services or simply because I'm me. So by using Business Style Awareness, I "slotted" with the team and referred to them as engineers.

Once they discovered their own business style through use of the profiling tool, eight of the engineers profiled as Friends; the remaining two were Thinkers. As we have seen, Friends and Thinkers are more deliberate in their approaches to selling. Friends are helpful and avoid risks; Thinkers are methodical and analytical. Both business styles are quiet, they ask rather than tell, and are dependable and supportive in their approach. This means they undertake lots of diagnosis and assessment of their clients' needs. Unfortunately it also means they fear rejection when looking to close, especially when they don't have a robust sales system.

The Pain

From a business perspective, Uretek was missing their targets, and although the business was in a healthy financial position, those missed targets would eventually impact on its profitability and result in some form of negative consequence.

Having reviewed what they did out in the field, it was clear that these guys were not controlling the follow-up. In one particular instance a large potential client in the public sector had requested further information to implement the Uretek solutions. But due to apparent workloads, not understanding priorities, and an innate fear of closing, an opportunity was missed. This was very disappointing for the salespeople involved, and the business lost a substantial amount of revenue. Worst of all, they lost the business to a competitor who we had previously established was deliberately targeting their market place.

Consequently, Roland, the MD, and I decided to review the quote pipeline. It was clear that a lot of running around was happening, the quote pipeline was busy, but on too many occasions the dates of the follow-ups had expired. At their current rate of conversion, there was no way Roland would hit his annual revenue objective.

We discussed the potential solutions. He is a big Thinker, so this took some time. Eventually we agreed a course of action to improve his conversion rates by training and supporting his team on controlling the follow-up.

The Fix

Controlling the follow-up is all about keeping the meeting's next steps firmly in your hands and under your control, as opposed to your clients'. This means that you can call your client with confidence — and without fear of rejection — because you have agreed to do so.

I attended a client meeting with Dave, a relatively new engineer/salesperson at Uretek. Dave was hungry to succeed and had a great work ethic.

Together, Dave and I:
- Delivered the magic question
- Connected with Uretek's FABs

- Elaborately told our third-party business-related story like Tarantino

Then I demonstrated how to control the follow-up. This is what I said to the prospective client:

'I appreciate how busy you are, and so am I, so can we agree when we'll discuss the next steps?'

The client replied: 'No, I'll contact you when I'm ready.'

I retorted: 'That's great, it's just that — like you — I'm either on the phone, customer-facing or in meetings, and I don't want you to waste your time trying to contact me. So let's agree now when I can return and we can discuss the quote in person.'

The client paused for a moment (yes you've guessed it, she was a Thinker), then agreed a date in the diary.

The client usually will agree because it's one less thing they have to worry about. My approach was positioned correctly, based on the business style of the client and sounded helpful and considerate rather than pushy and sales-y.

Back at the office, Dave sent his quote and continued to control the follow-up by finishing the email with...

"Once again thanks for your time and please find attached the quote as discussed. If you have any further thoughts, questions or considerations do not hesitate to contact me and I look forward to meeting with you next at 10 a.m. on Friday 5th June." Dave then sent an Outlook meeting request to confirm the date and time of the next meeting.

On this occasion, controlling the follow-up was uncomplicated because we had agreed the date of the next appointment. However, I'm a realist and understand that this can't and won't always happen. So what I'm about to explain is probably the single biggest change anyone selling can make to positively impact on their sales conversions — all you have to do is add a few simple words.

I have seen far too many occasions where e-mails containing anything from basic information to complicated quotes are sent without the next steps remaining in the control of the person selling. Based on my experience, most people end their e-mail quotes with, '...and I look forward to hearing from you soon.'

That's just not good enough. If you're a Doer or an Actor you may call your quote a couple of weeks later for some feedback or you may not. If you are a Friend or a Thinker you definitely won't make a speculative call to follow up your quote for fear of rejection. Case in point: the Uretek Engineers.

Without having previously arranged to make a follow-up call, all four business styles are less likely to chase the quote, if chased at all.

By adding this small and extremely important paragraph to your email — "... and If I don't hear from you by a week next Monday I'll call you around ten on the Tuesday morning for some feedback/a catch-up, is that okay?" — you will improve your sales conversions because you are now following up more quotes. Enter the time and date into your Outlook calendar but don't send an invitation to your client, and make sure you call at the exact time and date you said you would.

Please, try it. And as you've now invited a response to the question "Is that okay?" you are more likely to receive a response, which may include:

"That's great, and I look forward to your call."

"I'm not in Tuesday morning try the afternoon."

"I'm on holiday that week call the week after."

"Don't bother, I've decided not to go ahead."

...and the fear of rejection you've been burdened with every time you've missed out on that order will quickly disappear. In its place you will have the confidence to make your follow-up call and immediately increase your sales conversions. And all you've done is add two additional lines of text to the end of your email.

The Value of the Fix

Dave and I returned and closed the business, a substantial order in excess of £50,000. In the meeting we were told that if we had not made the next appointment there and then we could have lost the business as the competition to Uretek had been plaguing the client with telephone calls. As for Dave, he went on to have a fabulous year's performance, generating over £1 million sales. High Five!

In summary, the Secure steps of PROCES are only difficult if the hard work has not been carried out previously. If your Secure is stabbing in the dark then you will miss your chance to close your sale; whereas if you've followed PROCES, decided on your Plan of attack, delivered a customer centric Obtain, a convincing Connect, and a passionate Elaborate, the Secure of your sale becomes the natural next step. Consider my trainers purchased at the start of the book: all my buying criteria had been satisfied, so in the end it made more sense to buy the trainers than not buy them. This is how PROCES works, it "simplifies the science of selling", mirroring the psychological steps we all make when buying — aka Customer Transition, nothing more.

I completely understand some people not wanting to close and Secure the sale — it's your business style and fear of rejection. The engineers at Uretek, the solicitors at Hammond Trotter and all my other clients have improved their sales conversions by controlling the follow-up.

Following Line up your Secure are 13 closing techniques — unlucky for some — and tips on how to negotiate. By the way, I haven't used every one of the closes, but some of them do make me smile.

Line up your Secure

- Secure the next appointment while you are with the client and provide a rationale, otherwise the follow-up will be too pushy and sales-y.

- Add to the e-mailed quote the date and time of the next appointment.

- When there is no agreed date for the follow-up, use this phrase so that you control the follow-up: "... and if I don't hear from you by a week next Monday I'll call you around ten on the Tuesday morning for some feedback/a catch-up, is that okay?"

- Diarise the appointment and call exactly when you've agreed to do so.

- Decide your preferred close using the words, music and dance based on the business style of your potential client and clinch the sale.

Top Tips for Closing

I may have mentioned (once or twice) that I have been in sales most of my working life and seen all manner of closing, some good some awful, so the following closes represent just that. You'll have to work out which is which. However, it would be remiss of me not to share my most often used close; like everything else in this book, it is straightforward.

Before I list them, I should mention an often-quoted phrase about closing: "He who talks first loses." But common sense should prevail; if you have attempted a close and your client looks in need of some sort of help, ask them what help they require. However, most of the time I've witnessed a successful close, it's because the salesperson said nothing once the close was complete. So my advice after using any of the closes below is, once delivered, Zip it.

1.   Ask for the order

Seven out of ten pitches end without the salesperson asking for the order — of the three that do ask, two give up after the second refusal. Ask for the sale, such as, 'Would you like me to place this order for you?'

2.   The assumptive close

By assuming that the order is being placed you can remove the responsibility for decision-making from the buyer — use words such as 'will' and 'when':

'I will get the paperwork sorted and out in the post to you tonight. When can you get it back to me?'

3.   The alternative close (my personal favourite close)

This gives the buyer the choice between two alternatives, both of which have been chosen by you.

'So you can have the Ford Fiesta at £199.00 a month or the Volkswagen Golf at £242.00 — which one do you prefer?'

Why is it my personal favourite? Because PROCES always leads me to one of only two natural options to present to my customer, and as I'm a Doer I prefer this logical approach. But like I said, it's only my personal favourite.

4.   The pressure close

This puts pressure on the buyer through special offers that offer penalties for *not* placing the order.

'As I mentioned before, this offer closes on Friday and I wouldn't want you to miss out, so shall we go ahead?'

5.   The pen close

You hand them a pen and the contract while saying, 'Do you want to use your pen or mine?'

6.   The challenge close

This encourages the customer to make a point of being the decision-maker. You suggest that you are not sure who the decision-maker is by saying, 'Most business people in your position need to refer this kind of decision to their boss, do you need to refer it?'

7.   The quality close

You highlight the quality and imply that they wouldn't settle for anything less, so paying more is a privilege.
'We generally find that only the people who appreciate and are prepared to pay for the best quality go for this service — so would you like to go ahead?'

8.   The negative close

You create an obstacle for the customer, if they weren't to purchase straight away.
'I'm sorry, but due to the holidays we can't deliver in the three weeks after the 15th, so we can only do it next week. Is that okay?'

9.   The next to nothing close

You show them how the cost is far less and more appealing when they break it down month by month or week by week.

'Over three years it might seem a lot of money, but we find that most responsible people decide they simply have no choice but to go for it when it's less than a pound a day to protect your.../safeguard your..../ improve your... [whatever].' (Good for add-ons)

10.   The sympathy close

You tell them how desperate you are to get the sale and plead with them to buy.

'I know you have some reservations that we can't overcome right now, but I've got to admit that I'm pretty desperate for this sale — my manager says he'll sack me if I don't get an order this week, and you're my last chance. I'd be ever so grateful if you'd go ahead, and I promise you we'd be able to sort out the extra features once I speak to our supply people...'

11.   The puppy dog close

You say, 'Let me leave it with you and you see how you get on with it...' and then stand there pulling a face like a puppy dog until the client says, 'Oh, go on then.'

12.   The Columbo close

The meeting has finished, you calmly put your laptop away, place it in your bag and leave. Just before you open the door and exit the room, you stop, turn around and say:

'Just one last thing — would you tell me where I went wrong. I know this is right for you, so I must have missed something.'

13.   The elimination close

This is where you work through each reason why the customer may not be happy to go ahead.

The salesperson would say, 'I can see I've not explained this properly — can we take a moment to go through all the benefits and see which one is holding us back from proceeding?'

At which point, the salesperson lists all the benefits and one by one puts a strike through those about which the customer remains unconvinced. When you cross the last one out you can claim that there really seems to be no reason for not going ahead...

How to Negotiate

The question I'm most often asked about negotiation is, How do you begin to negotiate? Your business style impacts so much on your negotiation style that you may be less likely to negotiate if you're a Friend and/or appear too one-sided in your negotiation if you are a Doer.

So like everything else we say in Sellology: you need a system. At Kennedy Ross we use Negotiable Variables to enable you the salesperson, director or business owner to place a value on what you can and can't negotiate with. This means you recognise what's important to your customers and potentially less important to you, or vice versa. You can then make an objective decision based on the information you present. Either way, decide on the parameters of your negotiation — what you want to negotiate on, your price, your profit, your service, added value. You then have a plan in which you can recognise when your customer and you will have arrived at the win-win your looking for. As a result, your customer will always feel as though they have won when actually the outcome is mutually beneficial. This can only be done if you have completed PROCES

On the following page you will see a table that will guide you on how to rationalise your thinking and create the most favourable outcome for both your customer and you. A win-win.

Complete it on your own or with teams in your business — then get out there and Secure that deal !

Negotiable Variable: How to create a win-win

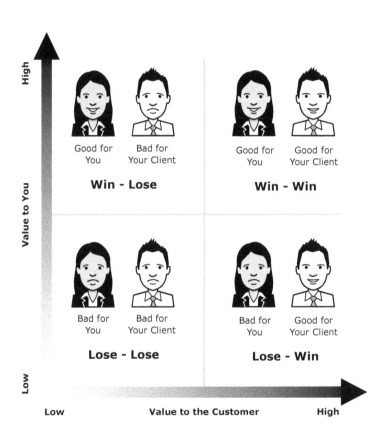

Now go for it!

'Chance favours the prepared mind.'

Louis Pasteur

You should now understand the importance of clear and concise communication in selling, i.e. words, music and dance in the physiology of selling.

You've tried out the Business Style Awareness profiling tool, the Psychology of Selling, had some fun guessing your colleagues' style, and most of all you know how to get on with everyone within the first seven seconds of meeting them. And you have a simple, powerful and repeatable system for increasing your sales fast: PROCES.

You now have all the tools you need to dispel any fears you may have had about selling, help you discover new opportunities for growth, and make a huge and immediate impact on your sales performance. As a thank you for reaching the end of this book, read on to discover how you can get a full refund on the purchase price.

At Kennedy Ross, we find that when we consistently do the right things, we tend to get the right results. I have only ever been lucky in sales when things are already going well, never when business is poor.

Why is that? It's because if I am already doing all the right things to get sales in the first place (i.e. consistently using an effective sales system – Sellology!), it's only a matter of time before the sales come in. Sellology is the key to creating your own luck.

History is full of examples of great leaps forward due to fortunate accidents that happen to people who were already working incredibly hard — from the discovery of Viagra to the invention of Coca-Cola. Alexander Fleming discovered penicillin after years of research, but his big breakthrough occurred when he accidentally left a petri dish out overnight. Was that a fluke or did the lucky accident happen because Fleming had been working so hard for so long?
Sellology is a bit like all those experiments that Fleming undertook while working towards his discovery.

Communicating clearly and using our foolproof methodology to Plan (both externally and internally), Reach out, Obtain the correct information, Connect with your client, Elaborate with conviction, and Secure the next steps, will help you deal with the single variable that is most difficult to predict: people. And now you have and understand how to use your secret weapon to overcome that variable: Sellology

I began this book by explaining that everything is done better if it is systematised. And yes I stand by that, especially in sales. But sales is also about getting on with your customers, always under promising and over delivering, and more than anything else, integrity. Without integrity you will always be a one-hit wonder whilst giving salespeople that bad reputation that I mentioned in the introduction.

You see, selling with integrity means your actions and behaviours will be respected and valued and your sales pipeline long and full. Integrity fills you with confidence, makes you strong and builds self-esteem, ensuring you'll bounce back when you do get the occasional No.
So this is it. Take a deep breath, make sure you cover all aspects of Sellology, practise, practise, practise, dive in and go for it!

I would love to hear about your selling success using Sellology techniques. If I use your story on my website or in the next edition of this book, I shall refund the price you paid.

Ali.jama@kennedyross.co.uk

LinkedIn   Alistaire Jama

Twitter   @kennedy_ross

Facebook Kennedy Ross Consulting Limited

Web   www.kennedyross.co.uk

ACKNOWLEDGEMENTS

There are a lot of people I would like to thank who have supported me on this journey. I'd like to begin by saying thanks to all the sales people and managers I had the pleasure to work with over 10 award-winning years at Thomson Directories, my initial inspiration behind Sellology.

To the sales and management teams I worked with at BT during those record periods of growth and then those who followed me to 118118 media, as well as all the salespeople and directors at 118118 media — you helped shape my sales thinking and made Sellology sharper.

Also to the sales teams, managers and directors at the *Manchester Evening News* through the perfect storm of economic turmoil, we brought the business back into profit whilst working with a smile.

Thanks to Rob Binns and the team at Cotton Court for the use of their office space.

A very big thanks to all my clients I have had the pleasure of working with, especially Janet Handley of SAL Abrasive Technologies, Eddy Fishwick of FISC Healthcare, Martin Hammond of Hammond Trotter solicitors (aka Driving Defences), Stewart Penny of

Ripple Aquaplast, Roland Caldbeck of Uretek, and Antony Morawski of Thomas Moss Fruit & Veg Wholesale. Let me make this absolutely clear: all of you have contributed to this book through your collaborations, feedback and support.

I would also like to thank the team at Kennedy Ross, in particular associates Neil Simpson, our social media expert, and my daughter Leyla Jama, our Generation Y expert.

Special thanks to Mel Tottah at Arwel Douglas for introducing me to Albert Mehrabian and providing me with the innovation behind the physiology of selling.

A big thanks to Ed Christiano and his design team at Deeper Blue, Malcolm Wyatt (journalist extraordinaire), and editor, Alan Whelan.

And finally, thanks to my beautiful wife Natalie Jama for her constant support and insight whilst keeping my feet firmly on the ground.

This book is dedicated to all those people who never believed they would be able to sell.

Well, you can now!

Lightning Source UK Ltd.
Milton Keynes UK
UKHW040632031218
333381UK00001B/343/P